The Systems Thinking School

Leading Systematic School Improvement

Titles in the Series

The Systems Thinking School

Redesigning Schools from the Inside-Out

Peter A. Barnard

ROWMAN & LITTLEFIELD EDUCATION
A division of
ROWMAN & LITTLEFIELD PUBLISHERS, INC.
Lanham • New York • Toronto • Plymouth, UK

Published by Rowman & Littlefield Education
A division of Rowman & Littlefield Publishers, Inc.
A wholly owned subsidiary of The Rowman & Littlefield Publishing Group, Inc.
4501 Forbes Boulevard, Suite 200, Lanham, Maryland 20706
www.rowman.com

10 Thornbury Road, Plymouth PL6 7PP, United Kingdom

British Library Cataloguing in Publication Information Available

Library of Congress Cataloging-in-Publication Data Available
ISBN 978-1-4758-0581-9 (cloth : alk. paper) -- ISBN 978-1-4758-0579-6 (pbk. : alk. paper) -- ISBN 978-1-4758-0580-2 (electronic)

∞™ The paper used in this publication meets the minimum requirements of American National Standard for Information Sciences Permanence of Paper for Printed Library Materials, ANSI/NISO Z39.48-1992.

Printed in the United States of America

If a factory is torn down but the rationality that produced it is left standing, then the rationality will simply produce another factory.

—Robert Pirsig (2006)

Contents

Foreword

Peter Barnard might as well have called this book *Thinking* because that is what he invites readers to do. It is time, he argues passionately, to set aside all the tinkering that sits at the heart of modern school improvement and reform and recognize that the problem is *not* performance. The problem is the linear system we are stuck with.

I have known Peter for twenty years and he has always been the iconoclast, demanding attention. In the early days when schools began to grapple seriously with data-driven reform, he was out in front showing them how to keep things simple and make the evidence count. He stood out as a dynamic leader and he used every lever to lift performance in two successful schools.

If you did not know him well, you might have assumed that he was steeped in the reform measures of his day, a shining example of how all thought leaders should behave. But even then, Peter was thinking ahead.

As I read this, his newest book, I was reminded of one of the first books I ever read as a teacher: Postman and Weitgartner's *Teaching as a Subversive Activity*. The book took to pieces the insipid curriculum of its time and offered its readers a blank page on which they could write their new ideas. But if you came up with the same old notions that underpinned almost every other curriculum they had studied, the authors enjoined you to use someone else's page!

Peter has the same approach to leading schools. A new approach is needed and the way to get there is by thinking afresh.

He first introduces the reader to a rich literature in systems thinking. Essentially, Peter provides the reader with a method for changing how we see the problem so that we might change the solution. By Chapter 3, he has adapted Seddons' Six Steps to a transformational approach based on what our customers—that is, students and their parents—want. Do not be distracted by the sound and fury that he lets loose on everyone who has not gone through the same discipline. The point is that he wants you to take the six steps and more, yourself.

And then, to help readers progress faster, Peter drives a spear through one of the main design features of the education systems: grouping students by age. The outcome is liberating. How might we organize ourselves differently?

What follows is no guidebook. It is a dizzy mixture of fundamental educational ideas—the partnership with parents, the collaboration of peers, the centrality of values, the strength of the tutor's role, assessment for learning—with powerful, new thinking tools. And then, for good measure, comes a windstorm of fresh insights from philosophers, social psychologists, positive psychologists, child development experts and, yes, systems thinkers to keep driving us on.

There are casualties along the way: Class size reformers. Toolkit designers. Those who argue, "If only we had a great teacher in every classroom."

And the final journey takes us into vertical tutoring, which gives the book what it needs: a call to arms and a whole bunch of great, practical ideas.

But, for goodness sake, do not treat this book as a template. The message is this: Let's get back to thinking deeply about all that schooling means today.

Ralph Tabberer CB
International consultant in education: formerly Director General of
Schools at the DfES and Head of the UK's Teacher Training Agency

Preface

Writing a book on systems thinking is frustrating to say the least. Each chapter seems to hanker after ones already written or seeks to refer to those that come later. Systems thinking does not like to be broken down into *chapters* and *headings* and prefers to look at whole processes. Neither does it particularly like rational order, and this means that chapters may go wherever they please; most have moved several times while others have ended up on the cutting-room floor. Whether the current order is right is a moot point.

However, it is possible to read most chapters individually. To make sense, each is wrapped within the whole-school learning process and this means some repetition. My personal preference is to start at the back of a book while college students tell me they prefer to *dip in*, and that all they really want is a bit of controversy and the odd quote for a thesis. I hope readers will find both.

I tried to follow the systems thinking process with this book, which involves checking the school as a system, gathering knowledge, and leveraging the changes needed to effect redesign. Such a process should result in a book that cherishes the management principles, processes, and values needed to create a systems thinking school. I always knew what the end-school looked like, having been fortunate enough to create two and to assist hundreds of others in transforming; the problem as always is getting there without being too boring.

Many readers in the United States may be unfamiliar with the phrase *vertical tutoring*. Nearly all secondary schools are organized horizontally as linear *year* or *grade* systems. Even school home groups or tutor groups are designed this way. In a school with vertical tutoring (VT), a small but highly significant change is made. Home groups—what US education calls homerooms—become a mixture of students from different grades or years, and

this small change, when understood at a systems level, sparks a whole se-
quence of amazing events throughout the school. It can kick-start a process
of school redesign from the inside out. Such changes, however, have to be
understood, managed, and values-driven.

Finally, a word about apostrophes. The word *systems* is used throughout.
This is largely because it joins up with other words to form complex nouns
and these are sometimes personified. However, there are many times when
an apostrophe might have been added to form *system's* or *systems'* and there
are occasions when it might have been made into the adjective, *systemic*. I
have tended to avoid these out of choice not laziness. It simply reads better
and retains a certain *systems status* if left in the plural form alone.

Please be assured that I remain a great advocate of the apostrophe and
mean it no harm. Any other errors are mine.

Acknowledgments

I should like to thank a few important and influential people for their support. In the United States, Professor Frank Duffy works tirelessly in the field of systems thinking and educational change. It was he who suggested that these scribblings should form part of his own systems thinking series. I hope I have managed to get somewhere near to the standard he has set and made a useful contribution.

In the way that systems join up, Frank sent me to Tom Koerner, vice president and editorial director of Rowman and Littlefield. I'd like to thank Tom for his enthusiasm and encouragement and for the long list of instructions and guidelines he sent to me—none of which I understood. It was Tom, probably exasperated by my ineptitude, who sent me to Patricia George to knock this book into shape. It was Patricia who translated the book from my Anglo Saxon English to American speak and advised me on corrections and bibliographical matters (some 2,389 alterations). I have learned much about the American use of the comma, a preference for *z* rather than *s*, and the solution to the practice/practise dichotomy faced in the United Kingdom. At no time did Patricia seem remotely phased by the task she faced and it was my good fortune to liaise with a person of such patience, wit, and ability. I hope one day, to cross the pond and meet all of these amazing people and thank them personally.

Otherwise, any errors that remain are mine and I hope none cause offense.

I should also like to acknowledge and thank more than four hundred secondary schools in the United Kingdom, Germany, Qatar, China, and elsewhere that have invited me to share time with them and help them change to a vertical culture that better supports and promotes learning.

This book is the last in my personal trilogy on school improvement. Sadly, I have no expert advisers to inform me of errors, save for my family who politely ignore me most of the time. My son, Laurent, continues to travel the world with his hard-core punk band Gallows and appears to have made no use of his degree in English. The other Patricia in my life, my partner of more than thirty years, is again designing a garden for the Chelsea Flower Show for the charity WaterAid. Once again, she is delighted that ex-Beatle Ringo Starr will perform the opening ceremony. Education, like family life, really is an odd, surprising, and joyous endeavor.

Prologue: The Systems Thinking School

> [T]he human participants in American education are the participants we shall continue to have. In fact, they are some of the most dedicated and sympathetic members of our society. No, the enemy is the controlling system of ideas that currently prevents needed changes from being contemplated or understood.
> —E. D. Hirsch Jr., 1999

When working with a school on systems thinking, and especially vertical tutoring (VT), it is sometimes pertinent to ask the staff who the cynics are. If no one confesses, staff members are invited to point to the nearest known cynic in the room. It is only then that I tell them that the cynics were right all along. It is the cynic who spots the paradox coming and who usually is the first to see the systems in which they are working as strangely flawed and somehow circular. For me, such good people are in reality, frustrated systems thinkers.

One such definition describes the cynic as "A person who questions whether something will happen or is worthwhile." In the United Kingdom, cynics who question the mainstream approach are invariably perceived as negative. In the United States, they are perceived as organizational gurus. The truth is that cynics are too often correct in their counterintuitive thinking. In school, cynics take the view that change never works and that the best course of action is to wait and do nothing until things revert to normal. As Peter Senge (2006) said, "Scratch the surface of most cynics and you find a frustrated idealist—someone who made the mistake of converting his ideals into expectations."

Cynics have the potential to be great systems thinkers because of their instant ability to spot flaws in organizational thinking, and this rarely goes well with school managers. They seem to sense when something they are told will work, will, in fact, *not* work. They see trainers as peddlers of snake oil, and leaders as hopelessly misguided and out of their depth. They see visionaries as deluded dreamers. Cynics tend to fall short in one area: knowing how to put right what their gut instinct tells them is wrong.

Systems thinkers are not cynics, although they may sometimes appear so. In essence, they are realists; they have the common sense instincts of the cynic but tend to look at the world as an interconnected place where all things are interacting at the same time. They hold in deep suspicion those who think in straight lines in narrowly focused ways. They tend to see disconnection, inconsistency, and incoherence where others see procedures, practice, and policy.

In one of the great books of our time, *The Happiness Hypothesis*, Jonathan Haidt (2006) set out the metaphor of the rider and the elephant to explain the duality of mind (how people think). For a long time we were able to solve complex problems of survival using intuition and an interconnected understanding of the environment. In many ways a systems thinking view prevailed. There had to be group cooperation, an ability to predict, and adapt and to learn from mistakes.

That was an age ago. Learning then was closer to the environment but has since diverged. We have abandoned an instinct honed over time and no longer trust our hunches. With language came the rational mind—the elephant's rider—exercising control over the elephant's intuitive ways.

As the rider and elephant moved from the fields and the farms to the city, the industrial age required new controls over time and place and allowed less and less room for intuition and instinct. The rational mind became control-centered, analytical, seeking of cause and effect, scientific, and dividing, forever breaking things down into small pieces as the chosen method of understanding complexity.

We have all been the beneficiaries of science and logic in the West and we have built mighty systems to share the bounty, but many now are hesitant and less optimistic about our direction of travel. Our well-being is not good, so we seek logical programs to fix our broken selves but nothing seems to work. When the elephant became tame and obedient to its rational rider, a disconnection took place: to the left, reductionism and logic, and to the right, intuition and holism.

If systems thinking does anything, it seeks interconnectivity. It wants to thank rationality for all it has done, but now wants to listen again to what the lowly elephant has to say, to retrain our thinking so that interconnections can again be made. Perhaps the journey was inward all the time. Otherwise, systems thinkers invariably tend to start the same way. They use shock treatment to shake us out of our overly rational malaise.

First up is John Seddon (2008), to give a flavor of our journey. Think school!

> If investment . . . has not been matched by improvement it is because we have
> invested in the wrong things. We invest in the wrong things believing them to
> be the right things. We think inspection drives improvement, we believe in the
> notion of economies of scale, we think choice and quasi-markets are levers for
> improvement, we believe people can be motivated by incentives, we think
> leaders need visions, managers need targets, and information technology is a
> driver of change. These are all wrong-headed ideas. But they have been the
> foundation of public sector "reform."

Vision is empty if it lacks a method to realize it. Seddon politely informs us
that we can no longer see the wood for the trees. This may sound a touch
cynical and implausible to some, but to systems thinkers such a statement is
liberating and perfectly understandable and opens up the opportunity for new
management thinking and new ways of approaching the way we work and
think and the systems in use. Once we stop accepting what has become the
status quo, it is possible to look again at our condition with greater clarity.
Unfortunately we are inextricably tied into not accepting and not seeing, and
it is this that poses the greatest challenge for systems thinkers; persuading
others to unlearn.

We not only minimize common sense but are overly fearful of our gut
intuition. For those inspired by their intuition who are able to stand back and
look again, systems thinking provides a powerful mode of thinking that
recognizes relationships and processes in rational and common-sense ways.
Properly applied it can clarify what is actually happening as opposed to what
people think is happening or what was intended to happen. In essence, it
seeks an answer as to why things do not work as they should and suggests
practical redesign remedies more likely to result in successful outcomes. It
understands complexity.

I told a friend, a head teacher in South Wales, about this book. "The
trouble with systems," he said, "is that systems are dry and rigid." He was
surprised when I told him that systems thinking is not the same as systems
per se, but that systems thinking is liberating, creative, and elegant and that it
removes the angst from the way people work. Systems thinking also harbors
a profound and positive view of people, their creative ability, and their intrinsic nature and all of this makes it a joy to work with. It is a different way of
looking at management and a better way of valuing and enabling people, and
especially those who live out their lives in our schools.

Margaret J. Wheatley (1999), another great systems thinker, described
systems thinking this way:

> Those of us educated in Western culture learned to think and manage a world
> that was anything but systemic or interconnected. It was a world of separations

and clear boundaries: boxes described jobs, lines charted relationships and
accountabilities, roles and policies described the limits of what each individual
did and who we wanted them to be. Western culture became very skilled at
describing the world with these strange, unnatural separations.

Wheatley believes that systems thinking can bring schools back to life, and
the purpose of this book is to help do just that. Systems thinking allows us to
take a shortcut through the paradoxes and barriers that litter the learning
world of schools: it allows us to absorb complex ideas and see them in quasi-
metaphorical and subjective ways that have coherence and a commonality of
understanding. It helps us to unlearn old ways and gather the knowledge
needed to create a higher quality public service culture driven by customer
needs.

There is always a balance of objectivity and subjectivity involved, but
such a combination is at complete ease within systems thinking. In this
respect, systems thinking has a strange quality: when teachers engage with it
and are invited to see the world anew, they often respond by saying that it is
all so obvious, that it is just common sense. They are often genuinely stag-
gered by common sense and seem grateful for being told the obvious. And
then comes the rationalization, "But then, I always knew that. . . . Isn't that
what we do?"

What people so often claim to know after the fact is completely different
from what they were actually doing before it. They assume. It is as if the new
perspective revealed by systems thinking was always their original intention,
rather like being reminded of something forgotten or discovering a cherished
belonging long mislaid. It makes us feel reconnected and wanting to connect
even more, and there is no doubt that this is all primitive and intuitive in
essence.

This book is concerned with the school as a system. I have in mind a US
secondary school or a UK high school if this helps, although the organizational practice of schools for most children is fairly universal. Schools are
places where teachers and students gather to engage in learning. There is no
immediate grandiose or revolutionary aim herein to create a new curriculum
of learning more suited to our knowledge economy even though this has to
be a systems thinking purpose once the school's revamped learning relationships are in place.

Here, the mismatch between school and society is causal to systems
thinking. The aim is to explore the first stage of any potential paradigm shift:
what schools need to do and be to achieve the preparatory thinking best able
to change both what they do and how they operate. The learning process
ideas set out here indicate how such a paradigm might evolve at a fast pace
from inside (the school) to out, from the base upward, intrinsically rather

than extrinsically driven. This usually works well when fanning flames—something I hope this third (and final) book might do.

The immediate aim is to invite the many talented and amazing people who inhabit our schools to stand back a little and look again at how the school works as a learning process, to see what is actually happening as opposed to what so many think and assume is happening. This involves assessing why we are where we are and seeking out the knowledge, values, and management principles needed to transform both what schools do and how they operate—in effect, to put schools and our teachers back in touch with their real purpose and their value work.

On this journey, the intention is to use systems thinking to make it possible to more accurately gauge why schools are the subject of so much concern not of their making. There is much that is wrong and it seems that schools are immune to any governmental fix. Therein is the systems paradox: it so often appears that the medicine applied to schools to make them work better is the stuff that is actually poisoning them.

Using systems thinking to construct a better school process is challenging but fun, and several schools have made part of the journey. It has been my good fortune (perhaps, quirky nature) to be the accidental boss of two such systems thinking schools. One has long returned to the factory model! The other continues to be a paragon of systems thinking as a mature VT school.

To become a school principal required a selection process, and to be selected I had to pretend compliance to a system that could never operate properly and to adopt an educational management language that made no substantive or operational sense. I had to silence the elephant on which I relied to have the chance of making some small difference. I had to pretend to believe in appraisal, inspection, targets, and a national curriculum of unbelievable complexity and join in the cheating and manipulation needed to push the kids over the exam line as humanely as possible. The school had to manipulate the system to maximize outcomes even though these actions took us far from our learning values. Our moral compass wavered and too often had to be ignored.

There are at least six service sector outcomes of complexity, or what Russell Ackoff called messes. I have adapted these to describe aspects of schools based on Robert Johnston and Graham Clark's 2001 book, *Service Operations Management*:

- Things never quite work as predicted, resulting in a range of unforeseeable consequences.
- Information is lost in the system or is not accessible, causing reworking and delays.
- Misunderstandings arise among school stakeholders, leading to mistakes (failure demand).

- Information needed is rarely complete, so people operate with best-bet assumptions.
- Work is skimped and dodged, and cheating occurs, but the school carries on regardless.
- Job specifications become overly complex, causing work difficulties and group silos to develop.

All of these issues and more will crop up as we journey on. In noting what schools do to organize and manage a learning process and to improve, systems thinking (personified) will examine the learning–work relationships in play in and around schools.

In so doing, it will include the important and related subsystems of the child and the family. The book attempts to offer insights into how the totality of the school's learning operation works, including any values, beliefs, and assumptions in play. It seeks an answer as to why, after so many decades of change and so many thousands of initiatives intended to improve schools, we are still roughly in the same place and still facing the same organizational challenges as before.

Had I discovered W. Edwards Deming, Margaret J. Wheatley, Peter Drucker, Peter Senge, Francis Duffy, and others earlier in my career, I might have realized that mine was not a single critical voice, and my first book would have been far easier to write. I also realize that I would have been unemployable in the United Kingdom. In every way, I am still writing that same book about schools, teachers, kids, parents, and management change. This time, however, I intend to take the great management gurus of systems thinking with me even if I cannot do them the justice they deserve.

Finally, the book attempts to construct a systems thinking school. I shall aim for the perfect school, the only target allowed in this book!

As for the book's subtitle, schools are a wicked problem, and wicked problems are really tough. We cannot really solve them, but according to the late systems thinking genius Russell Ackoff, we can *dissolve* them given some loopy thinking and redesign. All will be explained.

Chapter One

Systems Maintenance

You look at where you're going and where you are and it never makes sense,
but then you look back at where you've been and a pattern seems to emerge.
—Robert Pirsig, 2006

Any engagement with systems thinking requires that you must walk backward to see more. You must avoid the siren call of the existing system that wants to invite you in, absorb you into itself, give you a job to do, and make you part of it, albeit an isolated part. In effect, you must fight the human instinct to join its in-group loyalty scheme. You cannot understand a system from the inside; nothing can ever make sense. You simply end up doing your own thing and then clocking-out.

Being able to stand well back as a dispassionate observer is the only way for a school leader to see the big picture and to understand how the system really works; but to do this means knowing what to look for. Only then can the leader orchestrate the system's ability to thrive by creating the necessary chaos teams and interconnected feedback loops, the arterial structure on which the full learning process depends. Seeing is rarely believing when it comes to schools. Seeing requires knowledge of where to look and what to seek besides squinting again at the things we do not really notice but that have been there forever.

Apply too much control and the system fails to grow and becomes a replica of itself, stuck in time, moribund and unable to adapt to a changing environment (high in passive dependence). The actors lose sight of who they are, creativity is stifled, and the school becomes a cliché of itself. Apply too little control and energy escapes from everywhere. Purpose goes AWOL and eventually the school starts to fold in on itself. Either way, the learning and teaching process is limited.

All systems change; their destiny should be to transform and adapt, to be ecologically in tune. Schools, however, seem to have developed a survival instinct, a self-protective enduring quality as a means of resisting change. They have become more closed than open as systems and this makes change long overdue. The longer the wait, the more cataclysmic it will be, so sooner rather than later is good! Schools also have a chameleon-like quality: they often appear to be adaptive, to blend in, but it is only skin deep, an evolutionary skill developed to avoid constant predatory attacks.

Soon, a child system joins a school system. This is the beginning of the organized learning journey that requires social and psychological know-how to make the trip. Progress will be far from straightforward. The school system beckons and the family system begins to let go. An accelerated learning system will soon be in play and new process interconnections will need to be made. Complexity will start to exponentially increase.

Ivan Illich was a great systems thinker, though he is too seldom recognized as such. In the 1970s he wrote a series of books, one of which, *Deschooling Society*, reflects much of the style and rhetoric of systems thinkers. "Many students . . . intuitively know what schools do for them. They school them to confuse process and substance. Once blurred, a new logic is assumed. . . ." For Illich, this *new logic* is a betrayal of value built on assumption and involves the child being taught to confuse teaching with learning, grade advancement with education, and diplomas with competence. He showed how schools tend to work in ways that somehow result in a reversal of their original purpose as values become misaligned within the learning process. What is assumed is not necessarily what is.

In many ways, little has changed. Schooling is hugely wasteful of talent while purpose remains uncertain, but no fault can really be attached directly to schools for why they are like they are. When systems collide in unexpected ways, there are always unintended consequences. Dismantling the causal pathology of political ideology, misjudged leadership and management training, and the constant deluge of new demands and ideas, including misinterpreted research, is not easy and especially so when working at full capacity; the school either fails under the weight or closes in on itself or both.

There is now a large army of people working off the back of a school system and most are making it weaker not stronger. But that does not mean that nothing can be done. By applying systems thinking to schools as organizations, it should be possible to see inside those hidden places where assumptions linger and to ask the questions that can enable schools to work better. Such a combination should help us think more about school purpose and function and the role of our schools in improving outcomes and contributing to the common good.

Patterns are useful. When a pattern of unwanted behavior is repeated, it is sensible to break the pattern through intervention before it becomes habitual, and this applies not only to kids but also to schools as organizations and to the many failed attempts at school improvement. Patterns are useful insofar as they enable understanding, better research, and analysis.

The full title of Robert Pirsig's 2006 book is often shortened. Its complete title is *Zen and the Art of Motorcycle Maintenance: An Inquiry into Values*. This philosophical journey of the rider and his *mental* motorbike teaches much about the process of systems maintenance and what is often referred to as *the metaphysics of quality*. In essence, zen is a philosophical inquiry into values. It is a book we all read when we were far too young and only vaguely understood when we were too old.

In fact there are two riders. The narrator maintains his older machine with loving care; the other rider (his son) trusts to luck with his new machine and when things inevitably go wrong, endures the frustration of requiring someone else to fix it. One has mechanical systems management knowledge and is able to *tune in* and understand the full rhythmic nature of the engine working: he can almost sense what is wrong and what is needed and knows where to look. He constantly attends to the process of systems maintenance, understanding how each part cannot function without the other component parts also functioning optimally.

The process of systems maintenance is ongoing, forever seeking harmony and knowledge in every sense. The other rider's main concern is to replace any broken part with a new component and to get to the target destination as soon as possible. Broken bits can be discarded. For one rider, the journey and the harmony of the system that gets him there are all important. For the other, the destination and that graceful harmony that comes from an inner sense of well-being is never achieved.

One rider has a systems thinking outlook on life whereby everything needs to be joined up, interconnected—almost a life quality issue—and the other less so. The journey for the systems thinker is an inner journey, a learning journey, a journey in and of itself; quality built in, not added on; intrinsic. We start our life journey connecting things, figuring out how things work only to find them being slowly disassembled and broken down until a time is reached when no one can work out how to put the parts back together again, and many do not want to and do not see the life quality point.

Schools, especially in the United States and the United Kingdom, are on a similar journey. Our teachers and our children work in systems that are prone to breakdown, that never quite do what is needed, and that require constant fixing. It seems we are always trying to repair them and that nothing ever gets properly resolved. School systems never seem to work properly in extended time. Our teachers are part of the working dynamics that comprise a school but too often tend to be viewed as just another component, too easily worn out and in need of repair and replacement.

Jurisdictions in the West provide constant *fixes* as recommended by politicians, think tanks, and dubious advisers that never seem to quite work, especially in complex societies like the United States and the United Kingdom. The school is then left to try and pick up the pieces, to somehow rediscover and resolve the link between what schools believe and assume they do and the values that they hope will make a difference. They fail to notice the qualitative separation between the two.

The school as an organization strives to be holistic, to have a complete operational focus on the learning and teaching journeys being undertaken, but the constant addition of new reforms, demands, and specifications keeps separating the learning process from the value process when in essence they should be the same. Simply adding new parts to broken systems never works and usually contributes mightily to more breakdowns. The failure is in our inability to see the school through a systems thinking lens as a complete and interconnected operational learning system rather than as a set of component parts.

Systems thinking seeks to examine how complete systems work and interrelate in ways that ensure compatibility between the work being done and the human values that guide the process. As such, systems thinking assumes nothing and is delightfully simple. It helps to be a simple person— the simpler the better. Within its penchant for analysis, systems thinking confronts the inherent beliefs and assumptions that cause organizations to break down and not do what they are supposed to do.

It asks how work works, how complexity is managed, and starts by questioning any accepted organizational practices of prevailing orthodoxy. Systems thinking can then suggest changes usually based on the redefinition and redesign of human working relationships within the school and between school and home. Systems thinking seeks coherence and joined-up thinking based on the knowledge gained from systems analysis. Some call this common sense. In effect, systems thinking notes the nature of complexity that broken systems accumulate and seeks to redesign the system in ways in which complexity can be harnessed and used creatively to achieve better purposes.

Schools share all sorts of common management and operational assumptions and practices in the way they work despite the uniqueness each has. Given such a wide breadth of schools, it is reasonable to ask how common organizational behaviors actually work within the presumed purposes they share. How, for example, do the systems in play cope with the huge variety of intake and customer demand they face, and how do schools contribute to a knowledge society? This makes schools fair game for putting them under the lens of systems thinking.

I am conscious that all of this may sound a little vague and metaphysical to those new to the challenge of systems thinking given that there have been a zillion failed attempts to reform schools. Pirsig described metaphysics as a restaurant where they give you a thirty-thousand-page menu and no food! He used to be a teacher so he would have read a school improvement manual or two. The fact is that systems thinking can return schools to a much simpler and more purposeful state where quality is built in, not added on—to a school driven by values and the ability to make the world a better place. In the systems thinking restaurant, you actually get served.

A mechanic was working on a car when he noticed that one of his customers, a famous heart surgeon, had arrived in the waiting room.

"Hey," the mechanic said, walking into the waiting area. "I've just fixed your car. I replaced your valves, plugs and tappets, tuned the carburetor, and got the engine running beautifully. She's running perfectly now. Tell me, as I do exactly the same repair jobs that you do, how come you earn so much more than me?"

The heart surgeon thought about this. "Ah!" he replied, "That's a good question. But can you fix the car while the engine's still running?"

That's systems thinking too; school managers need to be heart surgeons, not mechanics.

Chapter Two

A Systems Thinking Approach

> The educational system is not dedicated to produce learning by students, but teaching by teachers—and teaching is a major obstruction to learning.
>
> —Russell Ackoff, 1999

Russell Ackoff's passing in October 2009 at age ninety was a huge loss to systems thinking. The United States seems more able than most to breed such amazing lateral thinkers who are willing to confront orthodoxy by producing a turn of phrase of astonishing clarity. Gore Vidal was another truly great systems thinker from what he sometimes called *the United States of Amnesia*, and his passing also presents a great systems thinking loss (Vidal 2004).

If, as Ackoff says, teaching is a major barrier to learning, what about all the other paraphernalia that surrounds teaching that teachers have to use, such as targets, tests, levels, and grades? Systems thinking should always seek out barriers that prevent work from being at least doable and purposeful. In a speech at the Villanova Conference, celebrating his eightieth birthday, Ackoff (1999) posed the following statement and provided the answer:

> The best thing that can be done to a problem is to solve it. False: the best thing that can be done to a problem is to dissolve it, to redesign the entity that has it or its environment so as to eliminate the problem. Such a design incorporates common sense and research, and increases our learning more than trial-and-error or scientific research alone can.

In complex societies such as the United States and the United Kingdom, where outcomes fail to match effort and finance *in*, teachers and schools are both seen as a problem. In other countries such as Finland and countries high in Programme for International Student Assessment (PISA) rankings, schools and teachers are not seen as a problem. Teachers there, it is assumed,

7

are more effective than our teachers! Therefore, it is assumed, there must be something wrong with our teachers: a training issue, a personnel issue, a competency issue, an incentive issue, or a combination of issues. The problem is surely teacher quality! However, if systems thinking teaches us one thing, it is never to accept the accepted answer!

We think we can solve this *obvious* problem, and massive efforts are applied to this task with minor effect. Politicians even think that teachers in the private sector are better than those in the state sector. A minister in the United Kingdom recently commented that 50 percent of the country's medalists in the 2012 Olympics came from the private school sector (around 8 percent of all UK school students). The fact that the public schools have no boats, horses, swimming pools or armies of sports coaches, and top-class facilities seems to have escaped him.

So, rather than solve what seems to be an obvious teacher quality problem, it is better to dissolve it as Ackoff suggests. When problems are *dissolved*—seen as part of a wider cultural mix from a systems thinking perspective—it sometimes turns out that the original problem was not quite what it seemed. Besides, having seen teachers across the world, I believe ours in the West easily stand in comparison with the best in effort, desire, creativity, and passion. This means that the perceived problem from a common-sense perspective is not quite what it seems. Systems thinking demands that we need to stand further back and look again.

One of the purposes of this book is to show how easy it is to redesign the way schools operate—at least on paper. What is more difficult is persuading people to take time out and listen. What is even more difficult is stopping schools from attempting warped cultural transformations such as copying other schools or adapting systems in ways that actually cause more problems. Such approaches simply trap them in one of W. Edwards Deming's (1993) systems thinking laws, which states that systems *cannot understand themselves*; an outside view is always needed. The dissolving process involves journeying backward and forward at the same time and rejecting some entrenched views and assumptions that teachers and schools find difficult to let go.

Individual schools as systems are not quite what they seem: when people (school managers) cling to old habits like lifebelts, persuading them to let go requires them to take a big leap of faith. Schools themselves are not as resistant to change as they appear to be; schools want to improve and do better by their students. But the processes they are coerced into operating, or choose to adopt, certainly are resistant. Peter Senge (2006) put it neatly when he said, "[T]oday's problems come from yesterday's solutions." In this way, we keep trying to solve today's problems with yesterday's thinking because that is the dominant industrial scientific form in school use. Because of this, it is necessary to look again at our schools.

Quite simply, we need to avoid separating the people who work in our schools from their modus operandi, the way they work in operating a learning process. We must stand back and suspend such common assumptions and forego any application of bygone industrial remedies. In particular, we must set teachers aside as being in any way a problem of quality, and look at the school as a complete operational learning process that includes parents, the community, and the knowledge society beyond. It is not simply a question of looking in the classroom as the obvious hiding place for things going wrong.

The way a secondary school operates is not straightforward, and the systems in play are not entirely of a school's making or of those who work in them. Senge (2006) tells us how the former tends to determine the latter; he regarded this as the first principle of systems thinking:

> When placed in the same system, people however different, tend to produce similar results. The system causes its own behavior. The systems perspective tells us that we must look beyond individual mistakes or bad luck or personalities and events to understand important problems. We must look into the underlying structures which shape individual actions and create the conditions where types of events become likely.

People do not normally go to work bent on underperforming. Most want to feel valued, to give value, to do something worthwhile, and to give a good account of what they do. Teachers are no exception. Teachers wish to make a difference; it is written into their genetic code. Of course, there are good teachers and there are others for whom their chosen profession proves inappropriate, who need to be *set free*. Systems thinking must seek out what is actually happening at an organizational level that may be contributing to any perceived underperformance and output distortions.

Some may suggest, as jurisdictions often do, that training and recruitment is the real issue and the solution. The problem is that wicked problems invite simplistic, wicked answers. But if it is the school as an organizational operation that is somehow dysfunctional and simply does not work properly as a system, how is it possibly to train people as managers and leaders to work effectively in them? And yet that, precisely, is what we do. We train for system compliance thinking we are training for improvement.

Many believe that we have the best cadre of teachers we have ever had, but trying to improve outcomes seems obstinately difficult to do. We still blame teachers and the quality of school leadership despite decades of interesting if fairly ineffectual work in leadership development worldwide. The danger is this: when a system does not work and becomes dysfunctional, outcomes start to oscillate wildly. Managers increase their management of people because people appear to be making a mess of things. It looks as though they are not up to the job, a quality issue.

Such an inspectorial feedback loop of misinformation is unhelpful and to be avoided, but it is one that has dominated organizational and managerial thinking and led to the mass bureaucracy of checks and balances that some call *deliverology*. People then protect themselves with unionization at which point things get much worse. What was already a wicked problem becomes doubly wicked.

In creating a teaching and learning process, schools have to recognize more precisely what they are doing, why they are doing it in the way they do, and where this is taking them. They must confront exactly how they managed to get to where they are. Only then is it possible to successfully disengage from old thinking and so unlearn all the policies, practices, and procedures they thought and assumed were OK. This gives a school the best chance of ensuring that mistakes are not repeated and carried forward into any new redesign process.

Unless schools are enabled to identify and *unlearn* old assumptions and understand why management systems and their endless fixes inevitably fail, problems can never be *dissolved* and is why most tend to reinvent themselves in the persistent way they do. Too often the same old problems are simply resurrected in different forms. Only by understanding the old industrial factory rationale with its myriad of meaningless assumptions can we prevent ourselves from producing yet another look-alike school and look-alike school principal. And that is a problem. We can see the industrial model; we can even describe it, but we have completely missed the obvious, which is why we keep reinventing the past.

Orthodoxy is sticky and has a habit of clinging on, ensuring compliance with unwanted behaviors. Unlearning requires schools to look back at the road traveled rather than just forward. This may seem paradoxical and appears counter to the *high vision* demanded of school leaders, but by looking back at a road strewn with good intentions and failed initiatives, it is possible to better understand how we arrived at the *now* of where we are. To understand what has gone wrong not only ensures that mistakes are not repeated, but allows schools to progress more securely with new knowledge and thinking. But that means change and talk of new paradigms.

Schools have to somehow *see* and come to terms with the idea that not all is as it seems and that many assumptions about learning and school systems management no longer work but remain endemic to our thinking. To confront the system that a school operates for the basket case it is, with all its illusory fixes and reforms, means exposing assumptions and looking again at the underpinning management knowledge base. In effect, schools have to unlearn the false rationale of separatist, component, tool-box thinking if they are to prevent old ideas and assumptions from hitching a ride with them on the road to school improvement.

First, they must look back, reflect, and unlearn. Only then will space be created for new learning. We must use a systems thinking approach and look at the school and how it functions and see if we can spot anything that may have escaped our attention; perhaps something hidden, undisturbed by time—something we may have inadvertently missed.

Chapter Three

The Systems Thinking Process

We are learning to see systems rather than isolated parts and players. Under the austere title of systems thinking . . . we are discovering many things worthy of wonder. We can now see the webs of interconnections that weave the world together; we are more aware that we live in relationship, connected to everything else; we are learning that profoundly different processes explain how living systems emerge and change.

—Margaret J. Wheatley, 1999

The basic systems thinking strategy applied to complex organizations, that outside view, involves checking what is going on and using the knowledge gained to redesign how an organization works and how to leverage change.

Any analytical failure in any part of this process allows an organization to continue on its current path, inhibiting the organization's ability to adapt to new areas of demand. Schools appear to have a strong default position highly resistant to change. The systems thinking check on a school is the most paradoxical and challenging part of the process and occupies many of the following chapters. Systems always demand constant attention. This is because the checking strategy needed to understand a school seems to run at variance with conventional objectives and measurable approaches such as surveys, tick sheets, questionnaires, and focus groups, all of which fail in their various ways to inform redesign. They do not leverage fundamental change.

The whole area is vague besides being complex. When an organization struggles, the first sign is usually a problem with the quality and quantity of output; customer needs are not being met and schools have many customers. To understand how a school operates is by no means straightforward and to treat this task as simple science is not the answer. What is needed is almost a counterintuitive approach to convention but even this is insufficient; we have

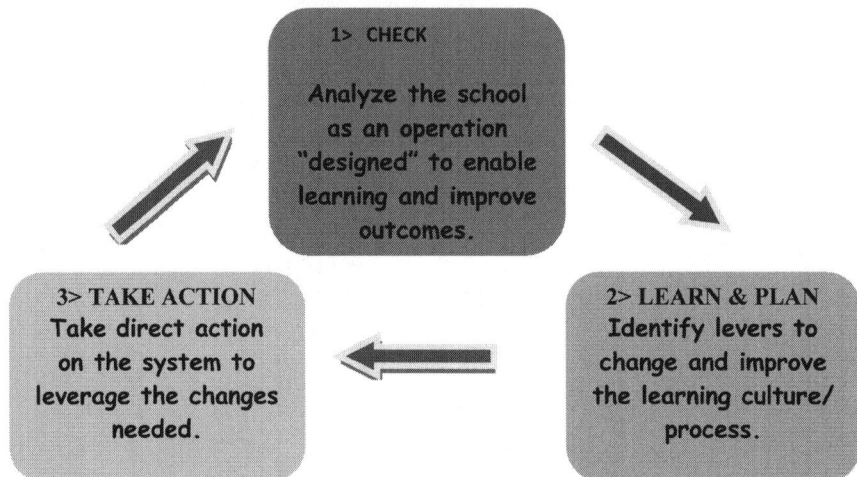

Figure 3.1.

to understand how our own common-sense intuition is influenced by our reductionist ways and is all too easily judged untrustworthy. So, how to go to school on this?

It is almost as if subjective comments and common sense are no longer valued and have been relegated or disallowed. Most of us quickly judge a school subjectively and with some accuracy without measuring anything. Even in writing this book, there is an ongoing fear of making any statement or offering any view without citing the research to back it up. A metaphorical descriptor or a subjective comment, however, can free us from a conflicting narrative of competing claims where one ideology competes with another. Our schools exist in a world of polarized opinion.

Systems thinking is almost unique in its use of subjectivity, but it still requires clarity of thought. As Michael Jackson (2003) says, not only should subjectivity be embraced by the systems approach, but "The only way we can get near to a view of the whole system is to look at it from as many perspectives as possible." We have to be allowed the luxury of interpreting what we see.

In this respect, the systems thinking lens is wide-angled. It sees traditional measurement approaches to system problems as traps to be avoided and ones that are more likely to make schools into prisoners of paradox than to free them to adapt. Surely, it is argued, if you are going to check something, you should look at component measures, such as school performance outcomes, school attendance, and behavior logs, and then put in place targets to rectify the faulty area ready for reassessment. It is all so delightfully and managerially simple except for one thing: it does not really change the system's fundamentals.

Such a remedial approach usually results in temporary fixes for symptoms rather than a cure for any underlying condition. This is precisely the problem: once you understand the system as a whole and appreciate the nature of the interconnectivity within it, the seemingly disparate parts suddenly appear quite different. Not only is there a need to examine the whole system, to see it in its entirety, but there is also a need to listen at the periphery to the language and scripts used by the actors.

The best way to approach the school check is from a state of ignorance. It is to ask the school management teams some simple questions: What is the school trying to do and for what purpose? How is it setting about these tasks? Why is it doing these things in the way it does? Such playful systems sophistry quickly reveals any values, beliefs, and assumptions in play and provides a first assessment of organizational congruence and what passes as systems knowledge. But you still have to know where to look and what to listen for.

The checking process reveals myriad school practices, policies, and procedures. The next task is to find out how these practices work together to achieve the school's learning purposes and beliefs, and here, schools usually have many bases to cover in a world of increasing demand. This accumulates information, but creating a usable picture requires the knowledge gathered to be set into a coherent framework of psychology and customer care. Within these two embracing areas, it is possible to compare what the school assumes it is doing with what it actually is doing, given the knowledge gained.

CHECKING

We can adapt the six-step public systems check set out by John Seddon (2008). By looking at the school as a service organization from a customer perspective, it sheds light on the organization's ability to supply what is needed, the value work. Problems arise almost immediately. The process of progressive steps each dependent on the previous steps may be adapted for schools as follows:

- **Step one:** Establish the purpose of schooling from the customers' perspective. The idea here is to seek what is of value to the customer and should be explored from the point of view of the school student, the main caregiver, and society at large. It is an important question usually lost in a world of assumption and discussions never had, but there is a commonality that should shine through. We want the best for our kids. We want them taught well and to be able to learn and develop their talents. Parents want to help schools with the learning process. We want a better, safer world and better opportunities for our kids. The purpose of schools is to deliver what is of value and substance and that means defining what matters. Unless there is agreement on purpose, running an organization like a school is a tricky business.

- **Step two:** Ascertain the nature and frequency of customer demand. This requires the school to examine all points of customer contact and to find out what is of value, what matters. The school has to understand what is of value; for example, how communication and information sharing might be improved. Unless the school knows what is of value and what goes wrong (failure demand arising from complaints, mistakes, etc.), it cannot plan and predict outcomes. Schools operate as information systems, not communication systems. Information sent home or made publicly available is limited, while information return is severely restricted. It is actually uncertain whether any valid means exists to ascertain what is of value given the confusion of purposes and the nature of the school as an organization.

- **Step three:** Find out how well the school is able to meet customer demand, to deliver what matters. This involves understanding the school's organizational capability in areas not normally measured, and this usually throws up a completely different picture of operational working. This includes customer care matters such as the school's ability to respond to demand, flexibility in learning support, speed in behavioral intervention, the effectiveness of home–school partnerships on learning, and communication matters. There are many others. Again, these are complex and joined-up matters linked to a more complete view of learning as a school- and community-wide process.

- **Step four:** Discover how well the school understands the concept of *flow* alluded to in the previous three stages. A school requires a reliable feedback exchange of information among its contributory players to ensure an ongoing and closely aligned focus on achieving purpose. Blockages to flow are rife. These include delays, communications bottlenecks, back-office bureaucracy, role complications, lost or inaccessible information, misunderstandings, and more. The school is there to deliver the value work as defined by customers—everything else in systems thinking constitutes *waste* likely to block flow. Following the value work should allow the school to build and design a better learning process, and this means a system in which information is rich, useful, and able to reach everyone who needs it to ensure delivery of the value work.

- **Step five:** Examine system conditions. This is where things get complicated and rife with paradoxical and contentious matters. This involves looking at the myriad policies, practices, procedures, management functions, and process assumptions likely to be sources of waste that negatively impact flow. Within the school, the management teams may well believe that these conditions are under control, attended to, and improving. They may point to their output targets, not realizing that the targets themselves may be distorting flow (sub-optimization)! Here the emphasis is on removing waste to increase flow. And this takes us to the final step.

- **Step six:** Understand management thinking. If things started to get complicated in Step five, they now enter the domain of most concern to this book and to any notion of systemic change. Things are about to get *wicked*. The previous steps should reveal what the system in play is trying to do and its methodology, the methods in play, and the assumptions made. So far, managers may have been reading this with detached approval, but that is about to change. Managers may not realize that they themselves constitute major restrictions to flow and this is reflected in the beliefs they hold, the assumptions that go unchallenged, and an inability to understand and come to grips with the fundamentals of the checking process.

It seems that the orthodox operational school system causes managers to somehow separate operational matters from the values that should be driving them as they follow targets, procedures, appraisals, protocols, and policies that all too often cause them to see teachers as potentially dysfunctional, ineffective, and prone to mistakes. Their overarching thinking is to manage people rather than to create a system in which people can function—the system they are purporting to *manage*. In effect, they perpetuate the waste that needs to be removed.

A MESS

These steps are a small but important part of the system checking process. However, the school lacks the wherewithal to handle these matters and the reasons for this lie deep within the industrial legacy that continues to govern school management behaviors. Unless such matters are understood and reinterpreted from a systems thinking standpoint, it is all too easy to assume that these steps comprise more invalid criticisms of schools and our teachers rather than of the received system. The fact remains that schools cannot be blamed for implementing the only system they know.

The fact is that our schools are amazing, and our teachers, managers, and school leaders are priceless. They achieve considerably greater quality than school's operational practices warrant and manage to enjoy high parental support despite the odds. They can even make the schools in which they operate appear to function well despite the practices, procedures, and policies in use, but none of this makes it right or detracts from the need for changes to the basic industrial design.

So, what can be learned from such an initial check, the pointers that need illumination to avoid errors and to design a systems thinking school—one more able to be values-driven, higher performing, and ecologically adaptive? The initial signs are not good, and schools claiming excellence are not excluded from initial observations and the general comments bundled above and below.

- There is confusion about purpose, function, demand, and what constitutes the value work.
- Parents have to access the service at different points and times and so are almost entirely reliant on what information, if any, is sent home. Parent and school partnership is poor per se.
- Information cannot flow. Most is restricted to the classroom and stays there. Other information is dissipated across the school. Information sent home is restricted, one-way, and limited.
- Schools appear hyper-complex and waste is inherent in most areas, including management, bureaucracy, policies, practices, and procedures (internal and external red tape).
- People are unable to perform optimally. Instead of sorting out a better system, managers try to manage people because people mess up, adding to the waste by introducing uncertainty and fear.
- There is high waste in all management practices and no sign of removal. Waste accumulates and costs.
- Schools manage complexity by increasing complexity.
- Schools have to deal with ongoing and conflicting ideology and reformation pressures adding to uncertainties and waste.
- Learning relationships between teachers, students, and parents are organizationally limited, risky, and likely to impact negatively on learning, well-being, and development.

Of course, schools rarely see themselves in this way. Their perception is that they provide the best service possible given the circumstances in which they operate and there is some truth here. These six steps do something else of profound importance for schools. They should, when understood, change the way a school evaluates measures of success and help redefine or reinstate purpose, what is of value. In this respect, for the parent, teacher, and the child, it is the quality of the school experience that matters first, and this can vary greatly. For most, this remains quite high, despite a broken system. Just imagine what it might be with an end-to-end operational learning system that actually flowed.

LET'S HEAR IT FOR THE PARENT CUSTOMER

Parents want their kids to have good teachers but there are (of course) variations. The findings presented in the research paper, "What Do Parents Value in Education? An Empirical Investigation of Parents, and Revealed Preferences for Teachers," a study by Brian Jacob and Lars Lefgren (2007), may be surprising to some:

> We find that, on average, parents strongly prefer teachers that principals describe as good at promoting student satisfaction and place relatively less value on a teacher's ability to raise standardized math or reading achievement. These aggregate effects, however, mask striking differences across family demographics. Families in higher poverty schools strongly value student achievement and are essentially indifferent to the principal's report of a teacher's ability to promote student satisfaction. The results are reversed for families in higher-income schools.

This quote is added to indicate the difficulty of discussing anything labeled under headings that combine educational purpose and customer demand and explains why interpretation and subjectivity are so important. Suffice it to say, to design our systems thinking school there is a need to accommodate such seemingly conflicting views if it is to respond to such demand and variation. This requires further comment because any polarization of views will cause confusion, and confusion is not good for customer care, school managers, performance, and outcomes.

Somehow, schools have to make sense of the massive variation in the clientele that walks through the school's front door, and in complex societies this verges on the extreme. How, exactly, can the individual be known, appreciated, and supported in learning in an organization that was never really designed to perform in this way? It is this collision and paradigm transition between an industrial model and the kind of approach needed today that needs attention. Simply saying that schools have to change is not enough. To proceed, the operational systems that schools use require a little redesign. However, that redesign is only possible when there is a shared understanding that the school as an organization is flawed at a deep systems level.

Otherwise, schools will be offered all kinds of advice and reforms. These might include multiple intelligences, different kinds of learning labels, revised social programs, training in emotional intelligence, more citizenship, active versus passive approaches to learning, changes to lesson times and the school year, traditional versus progressive methods, conservative versus liberal approaches, real books versus phonetics, verbal versus tactile, ideological slogans and psychological theories galore, and so it goes on and on. All have value, but all need to be somehow managed.

This book is staying out of the classroom but has to note conditions in which managers manage and teachers teach and how this affects the value work. Somehow systems thinking has to barge its way through these paradoxical notions and the multitude of reforms to design something better, something that can help a school differentiate between common sense and nonsense, what is or is not of value and to make the school strong enough to say why.

The last word is with Helen Gym (2011), founder of Parents United for Public Education, who posted on the CNN UpBringing blog on June 8, 2011, in part:

> Many of those who are driving education policy today are fixed on a certain set of numbers and measurements that we're told are the way to gauge a quality school. But as a parent, that's not really what matters to me about my daughter's education. . . . [A]s a parent, the true meaning of a quality school lies in a strong child- and family-centered educational mission that recognizes education as a "process of living" and school life as "real and vital" to our children and families, as American philosopher John Dewey wrote more than half a century ago. . . . While parents talk about programs rich in the arts, sciences and history, politicians talk about covering the basics through a one-size-fits-all curricula.

Let us bear this in mind for the systems thinking school.

Chapter Four

Wicked Problems: Schools and Systemic Change

> Managers are not confronted with problems that are independent of each other, but with dynamic situations of complex systems of changing problems that interact with each other. I call such situations messes. Managers do not solve problems, they manage messes.
>
> —Russell Ackoff, 1979

The debate that follows may never have arisen had it not been for social change. The United States has grown hyper-complex in its demographics, ethnic diversity, and the social and economic division between the haves and have nots. Arguably, the presidential elections of 2008 and 2012 heralded a tipping point in a land where it is estimated that 25 percent of Americans today are immigrants or are the children of immigrants.

Were it not for the complex conditions in which schools increasingly operate, the industrial school model might never have been considered broken; that is, it could have been somehow *fixed* or adjusted to suit. However, while school reformers seek to do *the right thing* and make the broken system appear to work, systems thinkers seek transformation *to do what is right* to ensure quality, relevance, and coherence. The latter requires so much more than the former and implies a values-driven method of getting there. The essence of this debate in part is to shift the balance from reformation to transformation and how this might be achieved.

A truth is emerging and it is one for which we should be grateful. In complex conditions such as those exhibited in the United States, the industrial school model fails. It is rendered unfit for purpose. But it does not just fail in areas where complexity and social challenge are at their greatest; look closely and it fails at every level, even for those schools who judge themselves competent system winners.

The simple narrative that all schools can be fixed by improving teaching and teachers is a tautology that requires extreme caution. The method required to do this is not to fix the teacher but to first fix the school's operational learning and support system. Otherwise such a notion turns out to be both a paradoxical falsehood and a truth at the same time and simply serves to show that we need to look again at systems and purpose.

This chapter focuses on the perceived view of the industrial culture of the school rather than what happens in curriculum time; that must wait a while. There is an order to change.

Many call for complete systemic change, and understandably so. This chapter, however, seeks a pregnant pause, a moment's reflection, and a last look back. We cannot simply abandon the schools we have and consign them to perdition only to see the same cultural and management processes reinvent themselves later on. Besides, we have yet to state what it actually *is* about schools that is so fundamentally broken and which is only exposed when conditions become complex.

To date, schools have defied the deluge of reform aimed at them and yet, hidden deep in their industrial foundations are the important answers needed to design a better school. We must recognize that a problem exists and slowly begin to dissolve this wicked problem. This chapter and ones following attempt to set out what we can learn from the *failure of reform* and how to better approach any new systemic beginning. Herewith is most of what we need to know with regard to any new systems thinking design.

Readers will note that *failure of reform* is in italics. This is where care is needed. It is easy to say that teachers have failed to take on board the new ideas and methods given to them by reformers. *If only our teachers were more flexible and could see what we see?* It is less easy to say that the teachers are not the problem we make them out to be, that so many reformers have completely failed to understand schools as teaching and learning organizations let alone the consequential outcomes of the changes they advocate. Between these two poles there is probably some common sense. This makes for a messy chapter.

This chapter revisits the systemic change debate, reveals the essence of the wicked problem, and hints at its resolution. It is all about organizational learning. Although this is easier for those peering in from the outside, it is less easy for those on the inside peering out. All of this requires that we enter a grand and necessary systems thinking debate. Can a school inspire systemic change bottom-up or should systemic change change the school top-down?

THE SYSTEMIC CHANGE VERSUS SCHOOL CHANGE DEBATE

The initial analysis of the school outlined previously teaches us that the organizational structures that schools inherently use tend to disable and distort the means whereby learning relationships between key players (students, parents, teachers, and school staff) form and flourish. This is thrown into sharp focus when context increases in social and psychological complexity. The industrial model is all about the teacher and curtails other potential contributions to learning from parents and others in and around the school despite what schools assume. This goes to the heart of the wicked problem, so we need to understand what is happening and why this is.

In basic terms, the industrial system architecture intended to make schools function actually prevents and undermines the essence of what a learning organization like a school should be. Horst Rittel and Melvin Webber (1973) identified ten characteristics of *wicked*, seemingly intractable, and impossible to resolve, *problems*. Such problems are information light, contradictory, and exhibit changing requirements and circumstances that are often difficult to recognize. Schools as they stand constitute a wicked problem seemingly allergic to any treatment. They have developed a highly resistant biology to any reform, even in those schools that we might recognize as *good*.

Francis Duffy (2008) cites Bar-Yam (2004) who tells us that wicked problems can have no resolution and that any search for *one-size-fits-all* and best-practice solutions will be insufficient. Because schools are inherently based on a one-size-fits-all model, any attempt at resolution here does not bode well. Before we abandon schools, however, we should at least explore the nature of systemic change a little more and perhaps seek one final chance at systemic redemption. Without such a pause, full systemic change may simply charge ahead and reinvent what we already have: a system out of kilter with its environment, wasteful of its people, and unsure of its purpose.

The nature of the paradigm shift needed to move from an industrial model to a more current form has been variously described. In essence it involves abandoning a system that is standardized, time-based, and preoccupied with sorting to a model that is more customized, attainment-based, and learning focused (Reigeluth 1994). Our quest to build a systems thinking school should complete two linked tasks. The first is to explain why reforms simply seem to bounce off schools. The second is to show how this can be fairly easily remedied when understood. Although the remedy is simple, the unlearning and new learning needed is more of a challenge.

In other words, the school cannot achieve the full-blown systemic transformation between paradigms of itself; the school can only do what is in its power to do and this refers to the school's power to evolve as a learning organization. In effect, this means getting the learning relationships right between all key players (the parents, students, and the school) and doing the value work. The systems thinking school is the necessary preparatory stage to systemic change.

Those engaged in systems thinking want better school outcomes more relevant to the world in which we live and compatible with the twenty-first–century challenges we face. That is fine and unarguable. Systems thinkers also subscribe to the idea that systems should be designed to coevolve with the environment they serve, what is called ecological systemic change. Duffy (2008) sets out the challenge this way:

> From this point of view, systemic change is based upon a clear understanding of interrelationships and interdependencies within the system of interest and between the system of interest and its external systemic environment. Change leaders subscribing to this view recognize that significant change in one part of their system will require changes in other parts of that system.

Basically, there is an ecological disconnect between what the school system does and what is needed by the bigger system it serves. None of this is anti-basic learning! So we are talking about improving our schools to get the best out of everyone and be coherent with an evolving knowledge and communications environment while recognizing the crucial role of systems thinking theory and practice in guiding any systemic change. The difficult points of contention are what best constitutes transformational *systemic* change and how best to go about making the transition needed to upgrade and re-culture school learning in order to shift from one paradigm to another. What does it look like and what is the first step along the way?

The debate appears to hinge on two views: big systemic change top down (revolutionary and fast) and little system change school up (evolutionary and slower). There is a big system in operation in the United States that involves and embraces the totality of schooling across all levels and subsystems. To transform, therefore, the whole system has to somehow change. Such a view is completely understandable and compatible with systems thinking, and Duffy sets out a sophisticated and coherent plan to achieve just that.

The alternative but tarnished view is that transformation should begin at the individual school level despite the litany of failed attempts at reform to date. Without question, schools have failed to change and adapt. Many regard them as broken institutions and feel that it is futile to persist with them. The case for schools leading systemic change, therefore, is weak, but a revised case needs to be made just one last time with an additional insight garnered from schools that have changed their culture.

The intention is to show that these two approaches (internally driven, bottom up systemic change by schools and externally driven systemic change top down) are actually complementary but that one should precede the other as a first step. In fact, individual school system change should not only precede big system change, but may even precipitate big systemic change rather than the other way around. On the surface, however, it seems that the evidence does not really support such a contention. As David Tyack and Larry Cuban (2004) stated, "The school reforms that promise to start from scratch and reinvent education from the bottom up almost always fall flat on their faces."

SO, WHAT EXACTLY IS IT WITH SCHOOLS?

Despite the odds, school-based change is the path (the first step) that this book explores, using the organizational philosophy of systems thinking. It does this even though such an approach appears at first sight to break systems thinking rules by wrongly treating the school as a component part of a wider school system. In systems thinking, any concentration on component change is a contradiction in terms and simply causes additional problems to arise elsewhere. However, it is possible to nominate pretty much anything as a system—a school, a tree, a horse, a storm, a galaxy—so there is an excuse!

We can tiptoe into this debate. Is it really possible to promote bottom-up school change given its history of reform failure? Or should we concentrate on a complete and surgical system makeover, top to bottom? First, we need to understand why schools do not work as they should, not just at a context and content level (beyond their remit) but as learning systems in their own right (within their powers), and we need to know if there is anything causal we have missed. This means asking the wicked question, "What exactly is it with schools?" and then trying to answer the question! What is it that we may have missed that schools can seemingly defy all attempts at transformation and change?

Is it just school management confused by external reformists and their crazy ideas that has gone awry? Wicked problems should at least be *dissolvable*, but to do this we need to know more about what is wrong. This means standing back much further.

This is why any debate among systems thinkers, although interesting, may of itself be a contradiction in terms. How can there be two conflicting approaches, each frustrated by the other, within an interconnected unifying concept like systems thinking? By re-presenting these ideas it may be possible to show that these two seemingly different approaches to change may be more aligned than is realized and that the reestablishment of systems interconnectivity is achievable!

THE PROBLEM OF REFORM

The background to this debate is complex and ranges freely across boundaries of philosophy, ideology, politics, and psychology, and so to the current calls for systemic change. System thinkers seem to agree that schools need to change and be redesigned. Most of the inherent processes, protocols, and purposes of schools have passed any sell-by date, and there is no longer a coherent fit between schools and the families they servce or with the society we need. Schools *seem* to malfunction and break down; bad news proliferates over good news and outcomes are so much less in impact than investment warrants as attempts at reform inevitably fail.

Indeed, no one is exactly sure what purpose schools serve anymore. They appear to fail as relevant twenty-first–century institutions, and many are those who seem to have become exasperated by the situation. Larry Cuban (2004) shares, "For goodness sake, let us stop talking about the financial value of education and talk instead about human capital, about schools helping to create people who are fully developed as human beings and as democratic citizens." Interestingly, Cuban was arguing against the idea of schools being run on business lines and being *boot camps* for employers. But this is in essence the industrial model. It seems that the purpose of schools is becoming increasingly narrowly focused in a world where knowledge is expanding. Schools are turning in on themselves.

It is all too easy to give up on our schools and our teachers, but we are lucky to have them. The fact is, our schools are full of amazing people but despite all the effort, research, and support given, schools seem to be robustly immune to organizational change. Given many of the changes advocated, this might not, of course, be all bad! Nevertheless, they remain astonishingly resilient and seemingly obstinate.

We hope, for example, that new pro-social education programs will change risk-taking behavior; reduce drug abuse, sexually transmitted diseases, unwanted pregnancies, and violent behavior; and even create better citizens and a more caring society. We hope that new literacy policies will improve reading, that new approaches to mathematics will improve the ability to do sums, and that blocking timetable time or changing this or that will provide some desired solution. When schools disappoint and fail to deliver on the new policy, the different methodology or the new way forward, trust starts to evaporate and in no time at all the focus of blame falls on the school and the capability of the classroom teacher and their fidelity failure to deliver.

This, in turn, sets up a debilitating reaction of *passive dependency* as the school freezes and reverts to its factory production ways which is all it has, knows, and understands. This is, after all, the school's unchanging management inheritance. Schools do the job we ask them to do and we then complain when they try to do that job rather than other jobs! Schools are not the products of accident but of inherited and outdated design that causes an inability to evolve managerially. They cannot be fixed by fiddling around, something W. Edwards Deming (1994) called *tampering* and David Tyack and Larry Cuban (1995) called *tinkering.*

School reform has been a hot topic ever since schools began. The weight of years sometimes causes us to balk at the challenge of school improvement to the extent that there is now a deep suspicion regarding the idea of the ability of reforms to rectify perceived faults, let alone change management behaviors, leadership styles, and teaching and learning cultures. Too many reforms seem to fail, and some turn out not to be reforms at all but merely patches used to keep a broken system going a while longer.

The process of *checking the system*, *gaining knowledge*, and then *applying that knowledge* to act on the system to redesign it is largely absent, misunderstood, and misconceived by school reformers. Like those addicted to nicotine, reformers use patches, confusing these with changes; the underlying condition persists. The problem is that we use industrial tools to fix industrial organizations, and this merely keeps the machine chugging along in the same direction. Paradoxically, this actually makes *reform* part of the *reform* problem, just as the manager has become part of the flow problem. The tools we have are system repair tools, not system design tools, but these are what we are seemingly locked into using.

Schools cannot analyze their systems from where they stand and neither, it seems, can anyone else, so we keep trying to fix the bits we think we *know*—usually teachers and curricular programs—by (in part) applying business applications that have proved all too fallible. Any *single-loop* industrial approach to a *double-loop* organizational problem (discussed later) inevitably creates a severe systems blockage to flow at a fundamental systems level. Anyone who has experienced one of these *flow problems* will understand that these can be obstinate and painful to remove! Even so, removed they can be! We simply need to take another last look through the systems thinking lens and diagnose the probable cause.

TRACKING THE GHOST IN THE MACHINE

As things stand, the received message is clear: reforms do not change schools, *per se*. But does that mean schools are a hopeless case, a wicked problem, and an amalgam of messes—irresolvable?

Larry Cuban and David Tyack (1995) describe this challenge in their book *Tinkering to Utopia*, which charts the failure of reform to positively impact the US education system. For the authors, the purpose of schools has consequently narrowed and is no longer that which it is educationally and culturally claimed to be. It seems that schools exist to supply the sufficient number of bright people needed to remain nationally competitive. This results in a wash-back effect whereby educational success is seen as a product of passing tests at the expense of deep learning while at the same time being willing to discount the many for the few, as waste. It is a system in which everyone ultimately fails, even the *winners*.

Underpinning this is a school production line that is out of sync with today's world. But in our desire to compete in the international paranoia of the Programme for International Student Assessment (PISA) race with the likes of higher academic performers like Finland and Canada, the country's best means seem disabled. This is not only frustrating, it is incredibly annoying for a country like the United States, able to roll out hundreds of Nobel Prize-winning problem solvers: some 39 percent of the total and 48 percent of all the sciences.

It seems ironic to ask schools to produce problem solvers if schools themselves are a problem that needs solving. The fact is, we end up turning out too many people who are insufficiently equipped, less open to learning, and more dependent on the state to get by—not to mention the million students who decide to drop out annually! None of this is the direct fault of teachers, but it is the place we are in.

For Tyack and Cuban (2004), our teachers have already become the *soldiers* of reform rather than the *agents* of reform. The standards movement that drenches the US system in a regime of testing banality treats all schools and all students as being the same despite their inherent diversity. So, where to go? Simply shoving increasing diversity in at one end and trying to output conformity at the other does not seem to be the best systems thinking approach to managing hyper-complexity.

SCHOOL-BASED REFORM

For John Goodlad, reform seems to be merely déjà vu despite his long-held belief in the school as a self-directing agent for change. In 1984 he produced his seminal book, *A Place Called School*, drawn from a major US research project. For Goodlad, the classroom is a place where time is the most precious resource. "Teachers both condition and *are* conditioned by the circumstances of schools. . . ." In school, it is the use of *time*, not talent, that creates "inequities in any opportunity to learn." In school ". . . the *clock* is king . . ." not the customer.

> A student sees five or six teachers per day and is known a little bit by a number of people, each of whom sees him in one specialized situation. . . . Save in extra-curricular or coaching situations . . . there is little opportunity for sustained conversation between student and teacher.

Note these simple words with care; they are all too easy to dismiss in our desire for change. Their deep importance will become clear. For our industrial model, the use of time is of considerable importance. Not to use it in the production process is to waste it. Time must be filled; time is money! This means that for change to occur, time needs to be revisited and bent just as Einstein said!

For Goodlad (2010) school is the right place for any transformation to start. He describes the essence of the school in terms of time plus *learning relationships* and throws all he can at the improvement problem; schools for him are precious and each has its own particular ethos. It is his description of the broken and patchy learning relationship between teachers and students that is key to schools as organizations and to systemic change. All we need to know is why this is, and then (the difficult bit) how to cultivate these relationships back to health in a way that not only enhances deeper learning and better teaching, but also creates the conditions for easier systemic change.

There is a systems conflict, and there seems to be no basic organizational fit or systems understanding to address the matter. Goodlad knows we need schools that are constantly self-renewing rather than self-repeating. His vision is for schools to be able to achieve such renewal despite all the evidence, experience, and research to the contrary. Reformers see the symptoms but not the cause, while in the background time appears to be yet another immovable constraint, ticking away.

Sometimes, we do not spot what is in front of our eyes. Sometimes things are so deeply established and there for so long that they have become an assumed part of our thinking. We end up looking at time or the teacher as the cause, but the teacher is another victim of the crime not the perpetrator. Poor managers too often blame operatives for performance issues rather than seek any causal system failure. Their errant preference is to look for faults in people rather than in the system constructs and design that are more likely to invite dysfunction.

This theme, of the seeming abandonment of any real learning relationships and interventions between adults and young people in our schools raised by Goodlad, is one to which this book constantly returns. We must organizationally heed psychological needs or suffer the consequences of the tragedies in Columbine and Sandy Hook. How can it be that busy and bustling schools alive with humanity can produce such resentful loners? Goodlad is right to call attention to the importance of the quality of learning relationships. Inadequate learning relationships are not just a symptom of system breakdown but part of the root cause. They were never designed *into* the industrial model; they were not seen as necessary, but they are necessary now and especially so in complex societies!

There are many clues from the past, but most have been seen as warranting only superficial interventions and policy changes. Social networking, the media, poverty, and in-group loyalty are all powerful influences on the learner. Even further back, the James Coleman study of 1966 concluded that the main influence on academic performance lay in the environment of the family and in peer groups rather than school (another systems thinking clue). Seeking school characteristics and descriptors most likely to influence improved outcomes can be very misleading in any school system design. We end up on the same dead-end route used to describe leadership: a long list of traits from which to pick and the challenge of creating a system that promotes such qualities.

Somehow, systems thinking must be able to *dissolve* and re-culture a wicked design flaw involving time, learning, and people, and how these might better interconnect to form a more relevant operational learning process. It seems that what our schools are best at is resisting change and staying the same. But the fact is, teachers do not mind change; why should they, they have never seen any! If all of this is the complicated gist of the problem, what is the design remedy? Is it little school or big system, or perhaps another look at the nature of the interconnectivity that joins them?

The case for school systemic change (inside out) seems to be a hopeless case and most system designers have packed their bags and gone home on this one. Except, that is, for the one fatal design flaw, the one that no one talks about because it is there all of the time, built in during an industrial age, untouched by reform, immovable, the one we do not see because it is too close. We can delay the reveal. Let us leave it there sleeping, hidden for a while, even though it litters previous chapters and those to come.

THE CASE FOR BIG SYSTEMIC CHANGE

The case for systemic change is topical at this time because it is again catching the imagination of educationists and governments, always an oddly reforming couple when PISA paranoia rules and distorts rational thinking. The case for systemic change follows an all-too-familiar logic, rightly focusing on schools, their purpose, and their role in society. We are told that schools do not work because they do not teach the right learning things in the right way; that they are out of date and behind the learning curve; that one-size-fits-all can never be right; that tests are not a true test of learning. Oh! And teacher quality is too low; it is a coin toss whether to sack them, back them, or pay them more! Best to start again.

We overlook the question as to why this might be and assume it is largely a content issue for the curriculum or a problem with context, perhaps social fragmentation, a training matter, or pay issue for teachers. System reformists worry about these matters. They are adamant on one thing: whatever they come up with, any new paradigm should not resemble or reinvent the schools we have! Given that many have a good feel for a new paradigm, the problems remain: (a) how best to make the new paradigm shift and (b) how to avoid reinvention of the status quo given our failure to properly analyze even the most fundamental flaws in the current system.

Our schools still act as a crude sorting process while learning is restricted by time and measured as the product of testing (low order thinking and learning) rather than as a process of human development (higher order thinking or deep learning). We have a high waste system with an incompatible ecological fit. These features were set out in *Chaos, Culture and Third Millennium Schools* (Barnard 2000), and such taxonomies litter the organizational literature of business excellence by people such as Peters, Senge, Druker, Belbin, Kanter, and more.

Our schools evolved to cater for the mass production and assembly line techniques of an industrial age characterized by high command and control thinking, bureaucracy, standardization, and compliance with specifications. They are still moving in this errant direction and many more erratically so because of reform confusion—and there can be only one reason. The system must contain within it a deep and fundamental flaw that prevents adaptation and one that has avoided all of our system checks. We note all the many output distortions, the waste of a nation's potential, but not the common flaw, the *common cause variation* issue.

Schools simply have been unable to adapt and evolve to form a new paradigm that is better able to meet the Information Age requirements of teamwork, flexible problem solving, initiative, and so forth. These require a substantively different and more qualitative approach to learning and teaching. One might almost describe this desired change as developing a systems thinking mind, one that thrives on the interconnectivity of learning and on the dependency of a range of learning relationships and sources, an active as well as a passive learning system. This appears to require a different back-up systems approach to how schools might go about their tasks. To manage complexity, schools have to be more sophisticated, not simpler—but how?

PIECEMEAL CHANGE

Duffy (2007) is rightly concerned about what he calls *piecemeal* change and especially when it purports to masquerade as *systemic* change. So he asks this question: when is systemic change not systemic? He provides an excellent guided tour of the area. Systemic change can be applied as a term to all sorts of situations and levels of organization from a single school, to a district or local authority, to a state. Within and even across these administrative levels and jurisdictions, attempts at change almost inevitably disappoint as hoped-for reforms fade and fail to embed. Such an approach seems to make little sense. But the bottom-up model school by school also fails. As Duffy (2010) says:

> [T]ransforming a single school (or program) makes that school incompatible with its system. When a "changed part" is incompatible with its system the unchanged parts of the system will strive to overwhelm it and force it to revert back to its pre-change status.

It is a bit like the psychology of peer group pressure and in-group loyalty (both of which will later occupy an important role in this debate). This presents quite a challenge to those who still hold out hope that schools can and must transform as individual organizations to create the conditions for any new paradigm to start. Schools have to reach a stage where those who work in them can *see* the changes needed and have the courage and systems knowledge to plot a better course. If this is so, they need systems thinking support, not abandonment.

Using Ackoff's eight defining characteristics for system change, Duffy (2007) answers his own question: systemic change is not systemic . . . "when it focuses on anything less than the whole system." This raises another question. Is there any point in writing a book called *The Systems Thinking School*? Well, yes. Persuading a school to adopt a systems thinking philosophy may yet hold some hope for a successful systemic change process. Better to have schools on the inside than reverting to the trials and tribulations of the status quo. Duffy's argument continues. Basically such piecemeal change at the school level is not only insufficient for big systemic transformation, but it also ignores Ackoff's eight principles of systems thinking as applied to schooling.

Duffy (2008) realizes that the current industrial paradigm is unable to deliver what is needed: whole new school systems that are totally aligned with the needs and requirements of the Information Age in the United States in the twenty-first century. Duffy sets out the criteria for what this means using the four transformational descriptors provided by Eckel, Hill, and Green (1998). He then adds two more criteria of his own.

Thus, transformational system change

1. alters the culture of the system by changing select underlying assumptions and institutional behaviors, processes, and products;
2. is deep and pervasive, affecting the whole system;
3. is intentional; and
4. occurs over time.

Now add Duffy's two important additions. Transformational system change:

5. creates a system that continuously seeks an idealized future for itself; and

6. creates a future system that is substantially different to the current system; that is, the system must be transformed to perform within a different paradigm.

Duffy is adamant that the Goodlad view of the school or partnership of schools as the change unit as set out in *A Place Called School*, has been tried and found wanting. It is piecemeal, and piecemeal does not do it!

MOVING FROM WHAT WE HAVE TO WHAT WE NEED

It may seem impossible to write this book given that it appears to belong to that category potentially and understandably filed under *piecemeal change*. However, it seems that systems thinking at the school level has followed a route into a mess confusing cause and effect. It has failed to explain adequately why reforms fail, and this is why we need to look anew at our schools. As Duffy says, unless we can explain this phenomenon to our teachers, schools will find any systemic change difficult to accept to say the least. The last thing systems thinkers need is to be labeled as failed reformers.

When we look at how systems thinking is beginning to be applied in schools, it is clear that it is in danger of becoming bogged down by the complexity, albeit parallel, that it is supposed to illuminate and simplify. Much is being applied with success to the classroom, but it is the school as an organization of which the classroom is part that needs systems thinking attention. Systems thinking is not meant to merely make a broken system work better; it is there to see through complexity and redesign the system in play to manage complexity in a way that improves relevant output.

Further clues to the nature of the fundamental operational flaws inherent in schools are provided via set theory, information theory, graph theory, and general systems theory (SIGGS), the educational systems model devised by Elizabeth Steiner Maccia and George Maccia (1966), and to the 201 hypotheses they outline, but to two in particular:

66. If educational system centrality increases, then passive dependence increases.
67. If educational system centrality increases, then active dependence decreases.

For now, please just keep these system hypotheses in mind. It is appreciated that when read for the first time, they can cause a severe headache, but an explanation will follow!

To help us, Kira King and Theodore Frick (1999) can guide us through, drawing on their article, "Transforming Education: Case Studies in Systems Thinking." Again, a picture is painted of a school system out of sync with the demands of an Information Age and the coming of what David D. Thornburg (1995) called the Communications Age:

> Schools must help children become skil[l]ful manipulators, synthesizers and creators of knowledge. And since we are now entering an era of global communication and collaboration, we need professionals who can work on teams to solve complex problems. Society no longer relies primarily on factory workers, but on life-long learners who can think critically, solve problems and work collaboratively.

Although we have a good idea of the demand side of schools and of the need for redesign, we are still faced with the old issue of reform failure. As King and Frick say:

> [R]eform efforts fail because we lack the abilities required for systemic design; we cannot analyze the existing school model holistically and recreate it from the ground up. Instead, we often remain entrenched in our current notions of education and only tinker at the edges of schools, making minimal changes. With the grandest of ideals, designers often aim towards creating a new school that looks totally different from traditional education, only to find that the resulting system is very similar to a traditional classroom!

The wicked problem! This should not be a surprise; stick a teacher in a room with a learner and you end up with a classroom, but we understand what is being said. Again, it seems that the case is lost for the school as the critical agent for systemic change. But in this rhetoric is a further clue: *our inability to analyze the existing school model.* Why is this so in an Information Age of problem solving? It can only mean that we have been looking in the wrong place at the wrong system features, allowing the purity of systems thinking to be obfuscated by component parts that distort our own system thinking approach to complex problems. This needs closer examination. As I stated previously and repeat here:

> Goodlad saw the symptoms but not the cause. Sometimes, you do not spot what is in front of your eyes because it so deeply established and has been there for so long that it has become an assumed part of thinking. We keep looking at time and the teacher but the teacher is another victim of the crime not the perpetrator. Time does not bend and we keep trying to repair symptoms not causes. Symptoms are the distorted superficial descriptors of component parts (teachers and programs, leaders and managers).

The other clue provided by King and Frick that seems to occupy those who want radical change is, once again, the system's extraordinary ability to defy reform and to keep recreating the *traditional classroom*. We tend to see reforms as failing in their purpose because they seem unable to break through the entrenched circularity and powerful orthodoxy of compliance and management thinking that simply persists and persists and keeps reinventing its original form. It is an international phenomenon. Schools cannot kick their old *people-management* habit in part because it is all we keep giving them. Invariably, they seem to navigate back to the safety of some out-of-sync homeostasis of the industrial age.

King and Frick take us to two more vital ideas that are essential to any understanding of schools: systems thinking and school improvement. They use Elizabeth Steiner's work (1988), which describes an educational system as consisting of teachers, students, content, and context. These form the basis for learning relationships (what Steiner calls *affect* relationships) and how a school operates as a learning system. Steiner describes a system as a group with at least one affect relationship, which has information; thus a school is a system that builds and defines affect relationships.

These relationships are powerful, but when examined simplistically (without psychology) they tend to justify the current industrial model (Frick 1991, 1993). They tend to recreate what we already have—the status quo—and this is especially so when testing rather than learning defines the content and the affect relationship. This same contextual problem tends to undermine any ability to intervene rapidly in learning behavior because of time delays.

However, because the teacher is part of an affect relationship with a student, the teacher cannot be regarded as a *component* somehow separated out. It literally takes two to tango! From a systems thinking perspective, any focus on the teacher alone is unlikely to result in the changes desired. We have to look further back and closer-up all at the same time.

Now we add another force, the central powerhouse of command and control thinking behind the compliance structure, which takes control from those who need it to service those who do not. According to the SIGGS hypotheses, when centralization is high, *active* dependence is low. Here, active dependence is the power of those in and around schools to influence others, to have some control over learning, and actively seek out sources of learning. In effect, this hypothesis describes a situation where we do not have to depend on our own human resources or on anyone; it is all (content and context) provided, including programs, time slots, policies, regulations, tests, claimed reforms, and innovations.

The adjacent hypothesis of the 201 hypotheses Maccia and Maccia offer confirms this: when centralism is high, *passive* dependence is high. It seems that any external controlling influence, whether command-driven or ideological or both, has an adverse effect on the school's ability to function by limiting the independence of the school's systems *thinking* process.

In short we appear to have what Ackoff calls a mess! Our school managers manage messes. It is such a mess that it defies analysis and simply keeps replicating back to its default industrial state. But even though schools are comprised of messes, we still need to analyze them somehow and understand even more about what is happening and why these hypotheses seem to be so powerful. So let us try a different approach, a slant on the systemic argument.

THE BASIC DEFAULT SCHOOL OF LEARNING

Duffy is right to say that unless we can show good people what is wrong and that what they are doing is based on management assumptions that no longer hold, they will not and cannot change. As prisoners of the past, they can neither unlearn nor let go, so any systems thinking arguments need to be persuasive.

If a school is essentially an interconnectedness of learning relationships, as Steiner, Maccia and Maccia, and King and Frick suggest, care must be taken not to build assumptions into this notional commonality of thought. Any systems thinking approach must not be complicated by dependency issues that are themselves built-in and seemingly beyond the school's remit. This includes context and content. In fact, merely changing what is taught (content) is a bit like filling up with a new grade of gas. The engine remains the same and probably does not run any better while costs increase. Somehow, learning relationships, management of operational complexity, and time have to change and to work as one. There has to be a new school and organization.

There appear to be built-in assumptions with regard to our acceptance of how schools are viewed as learning organizations and that there is a particular problem with US schools operating as they do in highly complex social conditions. To analyze and understand the basic interconnectedness of a school means we should discount the things a school cannot yet control, especially the *content* and some of the contextual conditions in play. They can wait in the reform inbox. We must deal first with the basic system relationships and management behaviors that schools can change, given a little unlearning and a little application of systems thinking.

BACK TO BASICS

Let us imagine as systems thinking encourages us to do, that the basic unit, school, or education system is much simpler.

It seems to be that the basic learning default of a child is *systems thinking*. Young children actively seek out and make interconnections to understand their environment, and in this respect, are dependent on forging learning relationships (active dependence). Over time, the formal school system re-packages learning, robbing children of their natural openness to learning and their active learning abilities by downgrading their intellectual inheritance and their potential to suit apparent time restraints or romantic ideals. We so easily mess up the learning environment and the nature and nurture balance.

The basic first learning phase involves children and their parents (an *affect* relationship). The context is one of nature and nurture, and learning content is basic and defined entirely by need. The school is the second basic phase: a child, a teacher, and the parent. The school and home must not be separated (and industrialized) as they are now. To do so is a fatal systems thinking and learning flaw. How can learning possibly work without the complete and joined-up information of those most knowledgeable of the child? So learning is not separated but depends on the successful interaction and interconnectedness between these main players.

This early years' work is intense. Any separation of responsibility for learning breaks systems thinking rules. When we moved from the country to the city, we industrialized learning and separated home and school. We broke the systems rule and now we are paying the price. As our little school expands, other students join in and the basic system starts to grow, so let us not spoil it all by adding content and too much context at this time. The critical part of the school (the bit we broke) is the interconnectedness between the school's participant players and our understanding of how adults and children learn with and from each other.

To understand this, we have to appreciate what has happened to our main players. What is it about the industrial model that has caused so much to go wrong, the damage, the system weakness, the disconnectedness, the difficulty of rebuilding learning relationships, and the inability to evolve?

Think of this as similar to the big bang theory or quantum mechanics. In the beginning there was the parent and child; over time a teacher came along to help out. Later, another, older kid turned up, and from all of this matter and chaos, the learning universe began to form. We have our basic human system elements. This is the school. All are concerned that the child grows into a better version of themselves, that the child understands the world and can make things better not worse. It is in their and the child's interest to survive and to learn and thrive using what knowledge we have, what is important and of value: the value work, to increase *good*.

In the beginning, everyone was a teacher and learner; schools must ensure they still are. Of course this was all before we rented out our kids to the state and sacrificed our dependence on each other (child, teacher, parent) and created a *me* culture of separation. We need to avoid this wasteful, alienating route! In the end, having great learning relationships at school is far better for our kids than creating schools that turn out people who might eventually need a shrink or drug-dealer on speed dial to compensate for their inability to learn and socialize.

What our little school system really needs to understand is how the adults and the older kid who turned up later and made us think of the idea of a school, can best function and learn; how all can work together to support and contribute to the successful growth and development of each other. Many schools actually operate in this reasonably untainted, purposeful, values-driven, and systems thinking way, where primacy is given to a unification of what it is to learn and what is needed to grow and develop into a great person: our dependence on each other rather than our separation.

When we consider the school in its primitive and infant form, we can see what matters, what makes it actively dependent, and what makes it strong enough to ward off compliance and decide on strategies for its own ongoing improvement. In effect, this is the essence of any systems thinking school and exactly the criteria Duffy set out in his adapted six-point plan for the adaptive school.

THE FUNDAMENTAL FLAW AT THE ORGANIZATIONAL HEART OF THE SCHOOL

So what was it, staring us in the face, that messed up our schools, broke human learning relationships, and made schools too obstinate to change? It was obvious all along, we just did not see it and because we did not see it, we fed it with reforms and it grew even more obstinate distortions of itself. It is this:

> The horizontal or *year* or *grade* system of organization that defines the industrial model cannot flex sufficiently as an operational learning system to build the kind of learning relationships and processes to which all concerned parties must contribute. It is inconsiderate of psychology and customer care; assuming of values, and unable to cope with complexity (variation).

When systems thinking is applied to the huge assumptions relating to an industrial school model based on linear, peer, or same-age production principles, it reveals an organization handicapped by time, severely restricted by management and leadership frailties, and produces system output distortions. Such linear models can never build the interconnective double feedback loops that enable flow and bend time to enable learning. Exactly how this is so is set out in the next chapter.

The result of this *common cause variation* allows output distortions to expand. Over time, school industrialization does the complete opposite of what is needed: it becomes adept at narrowing its focus, packaging knowledge into spoon-fed lumps, sifting out faulty students for retreatment and repair as so much waste while unnecessarily expanding a massive job-creation enterprise at enormous expense. The result is mass delusion and an expansion of unwanted complexity loaded on top of existing complexity.

In our linear model, we have completely ignored the psychology of child development, of Johan Huizinga's *Homo Ludens* written way back in 1938 and the many subsequent contributors, while ignoring the other basic building block of organizations, customer care. The school has developed an unmanageable management system whereby the totality of its enterprise and learning relationships has been dumped on the teacher in the classroom. We have endorsed the idea of teacher fault rather than systems fault. We continue, in Ackoff's words, to "do the wrong things wronger" until, eventually, a wicked problem is created.

The linear model distorts and undermines every organizational and operational aspect of learning and teaching, but is the only model we know. Such linear systems can never do the value work needed and are dependent entirely on teacher brilliance. It is technology at work again, making a science out of an art, confusing special cause and common cause variation, using single-loop thinking to handle double-loop complexities and creating so much unnecessary waste. It is this linear model that has stuck around unnoticed and that has maintained the errant behaviors and assumptions that no longer work—the behaviors and assumptions that stand full-square between schools and the Information Age.

Understanding why this is and how it distorts the school as a true learning organization has to be understood first if it is to be unlearned and abandoned. What has been built is a single-loop, isolated information system in school rebounding around classroom walls and unable to escape. We have got knowledge surrounded, pinned down, bottled up, and force-fed to inmates reliant entirely on externally misguided programmers and disillusioned teachers when a multi-nodal information and learning feedback process is needed. We aspire to exams and tests rather than to creativity, wisdom, and any understanding of real values. Too often, we inadvertently teach our kids to trash the place in their anger rather than to cherish and learn.

The subsequent breakdown of interconnectivity is why our schools are permanently in the grip of hypotheses 66 and 67. It is why intervention and reform fails and it is why learning is at risk for children no longer recognized for the uniqueness and the talents they all have. It is why schools are stuck and reforms fail. We have simply lost common(s) sense.

THE ANSWER

Escaping this closed wicked problem is simple: all it requires is an understanding of how the magician creates this illusion (the reveal) and why we so easily fall for the trick (the delusion). All that is needed is for the systems thinking school to learn how to change its learning relationships and re-establish information and communication flow, and for people to get back in touch with who they are and to what is important—the stuff inadvertently taken away—and then everything else. The rest of this book explains the why and the how.

What systems thinking must do is not reject the school too readily as a piecemeal player beyond repair, but to show our schools how schoolteachers, parents, and children became isolated from each other and to explain why these strained learning relationships have endured in organizational terms. The industrial design was and is teacher-centered and learning relationships were never interconnected at any substantive level because there was no need; today, complexity demands there is.

Today, that basic model and its accompanying management thinking are even more deeply rooted, leaving the teacher to bear the totality of the system load, a return to the default industrial position. In societies as hyper-complex as the United States, such a teacher-dependent system is unable to adapt or evolve; the wrong reforms have been applied to the wrong problem and this persists as confusion based on errant assumption. In effect, the teacher is set up to fail.

So we know what we never really saw, the entity that resists, and the design flaw that systems thinking has revealed—the linear production line. This is the horizontal year system, the conveyor belt, the ticking clock, the management and leadership of nonsenses, the broken learning relationships, the separation of school and family, teacher and child; the garbage of grades, of good people working to targets and to tests, all disconnected not only within their small system but also from the bigger ecological system, all without purpose: all good people trying to make a broken system work despite the odds in a world crashing around them.

It was there all the time in the architecture of the industrial age. They built things well then, to last! The horizontal structure or grade or year systems can never properly support an effective operational learning process no matter how managers and leaders try and adapt it. Outcome distortions will always arise. Such a system prevents critical and fundamental learning relationships from forming despite what schools assume and despite schools thinking that their particular learning relationships are OK. The school has to understand why this is and how they were led into continuing industrial mechanistic management systems based on false ideas and assumptions about people, time, and learning, and then were subsequently judged on their ability to comply rather than their ability to facilitate deeper learning.

Our systems thinking, analytical focus has been wrongly shifted to the classroom, to programs, to romanticized reforms, and to leadership (component thinking) wherever we wrongly perceived the damage to be. The fault is structural, not human, in essence, but the fault has damaged everyone all the same. But this means it can be put right, not fixed; redesigned. If the system can be redesigned, people can do the value work and think about purpose beyond the leaning tower of PISA.

DISSOLVING THE WICKED PROBLEM

This should be fairly simple to rectify now that schools are increasingly encouraged to act more independently of governments. Schools have to re-learn the art and the values of self-organization, described by Donella Meadows (2009) as "the ability to structure themselves, to create new structure, to learn, diversify and complexify." As centrality decreases, surely passive dependence should reduce.

We must, before any large scale systemic change, get the learning relationships in and around our schools understood, relearned, and restored, and interconnectivity reestablished. We have to get the psychology right and be able to recognize every child as a learner. This can all be done by one simple change, a first domino of a domino effect. Instead of same-age students populating homeroom time, student groups of mixed ages are formed (VT) and these groups meet once a day for twenty minutes. This book simply explains why this is so and how such a small change reunites schools with their true values, child psychology, and key management principles of customer care.

This may sound extraordinary and too simplistic, but this is the beginning of re-culturing a school and redesigning its operational learning process. Such a domino changes everything quickly and permanently when understood. If we fail as systems thinkers to support schools' ability to do this, we take the risk that any ensuing systems thinking paradigm will be misunderstood and applied in old ways.

The linear model must become vertical. But more than this, creating schools that can systems think is a surer means to build any new paradigm. Such schools can only operate by establishing the values that ensure adaptive continuity and substantive and lasting learning relationships in tutor or home group time and with parents. Potentially, this change will allow a significant organizational increase in effective learning and support. We simply build a new system that supports the totality of the operational learning process rather than rely solely on the isolation of the teacher in the classroom, one that reunites all key players. Mixed-age homeroom time is the start of abandoning a linear teaching school for a teaching and learning collegiality capable of returning to our kids their systems thinking inheritance.

This small change is far more challenging than it seems and requires preparation. A century of industrial thinking does not easily fold and requires considerable unlearning and re-learning at a management and leadership level, but it is well within a school's compass for those willing.

It is precisely in the wreckage of disconnected learning relationships that separation of school from home and separation within school itself has weakened schools and caused them to be compliant, stopping them from being the schools that we need them to be. We need our schools to be self-reforming as much as possible, with no reforms added on, but a reforming and improving risk nature built in. Duffy calls this (Item 5 above. Eckel and colleagues pp 50-1) a *system that continuously seeks an idealized future for itself* and a system in which quality and change are integral and not added on. Only by getting the school's working relationships right, ensuring dependency on each other is understood, and working can we make the school's value work, and work better.

AND FINALLY, GOODLAD AND DUFFY ARE BOTH RIGHT

It is not the purpose of systems thinking to make a broken system work better when fundamental redesign is needed. We can analyze schools easily when we see them through a systems thinking lens as places where everyone, not just the isolated teacher and child, is engaged in building highly active learning relationships. All we need do is make the intellectual separation between what is needed (a system able to build and reestablish learning relationships) and all the management dross schools have been persuaded to garner over the years. This is the fundamental and most powerful thing systems thinking can do to effect systemic change. The rest of the cosmos can wait a while.

This book simply shows how learning relationships are formed and why and how schools can use them with great effect. There are now many hundreds of such secondary schools worldwide trying to do just this.

It seems logical that given the validity of the SIGGS hypotheses, systems thinking should recognize what may be happening when an external and mainly top-down reform system collides with a school system made high on passive dependence and low on active dependence. The answer is a combination of confusion, an inability to act, or nothing at all. Reform fails and school management remains stuck. To be enacted and embedded successfully, reforms require the management knowledge acquired through high active dependence and low passive dependence, the opposite of what we have.

And there is the reform paradox. Once the reforming center retreats, the school becomes largely self-reforming . . . with help.

Having

- damaged the school as an organization with regard to its independent thinking mechanism;
- separated it from its values;

- undermined its ability to build, maintain, and understand learning relationships;
- consequently substituted and transferred what's left to the content and context dumping ground and isolation of the child's and teacher's classroom;
- designed leadership and management programs to run the same broken system; and
- misapplied accountability and appraisal type mechanisms to suit. . . .

We are left with the distorted consequences of a centralized industrial architecture, horizontally handicapped, where reforms so easily hinder progress and spell failure.

The root problem is simple. The horizontal organizational arrangements of schools using year systems and grade systems alone prevent the essential interconnective learning relationships between school, home, and child from forming, and this inhibits the child's full and deeper learning capabilities. The linear model prevents learning as a complete operational process by breaking the school's essential communications linkages, learning support and assessment methods. Both the parental role and the homeroom tutor role have been effectively sidelined as pertinent contributors to the learning process, and this in turn jeopardizes the learner, the teacher, and the family.

We continue to sift and grade rather than listen and learn. Our students are no longer people but walking sets of numbers and grades in a system largely devoid of personalization. This is also the architecture that acts as a limiter on content and context and on the transfer from extrinsically driven studenthood to intrinsically driven learning. It is also the limiter behind what in SIGGS is called *homomorphia*, the idea that there are many different learning pathways and many different talents that can be used and developed to achieve educational goals. The problem is essentially a structural fault, not a human one. We have succeeded in creating a system whereby everyone ends up doing the wrong job wronger or not at all.

The change to vertical groupings for a short time each day is the start of a healing process. It is what such a small change precipitates that is truly life enhancing and school changing.

Thankfully, Duffy also set out the pathways to change: "The literature on transformational change repeatedly reinforces the need for people in organizations to change the way they think and act along three change paths:"

- Path 1—Transform their system's core and support work processes;
- Path 2—Transform their system's internal social infrastructure (which includes organization culture, the organizational mental model, organization design, job descriptions, reward system, and so on); and,

- Path 3—Transform the system's relationship with its external environment.

This small structural change does what Goodlad wishes for and starts what Duffy demands. A short pause in the day when schools reforge their interconnectivity creates time to ensure everyone is known and parents are involved. This makes school possible and allows the classroom to be whatever it needs to be. It also returns the child's tutor—the person who maintains oversight of a small cohort of children throughout their school life—to being the person that the teacher, child, and child's parents need him and her to be. It allows the double-loop interconnectivity to develop and guide learning; the same double loops absent by design from horizontal structures.

With guidance, the introduction of mixed-age or VT for a short time each day sets a school on the three pathways immediately and permanently. The essential organizational shift that VT demands is to switch from being a back-office bureaucracy to a front-office public service organization: all core work processes and support mechanisms have to be re-geared to the new arrangements. Culture changes as soon as the unlearning penny drops; it is instant, in the first minute of the first human interaction, when a tutor meets a child for the first time in *their* time.

This book sets out how this is done and at no cost! VT can go a long way down Path 3. It cannot change all of the compliance practices, but it can secure for those who work in schools a systems thinking mind-set and learning relationship interconnectedness that enables better learning and teaching—a system more able to intervene, support, and enhance learning and to heal and make a difference. As the school gets stronger and confidence increases, it too can adapt the original SIGGS hypotheses and take back the power to innovate that the center does not really want or need. It can journey along the third pathway and inspire systemic change.

> If educational system centrality decreases, then passive dependence decreases.
> If educational system centrality decreases, then active dependence increases.

When passive dependence decreases and active dependence increases, the center will let go because parents will demand that their kids' teachers be left alone to do the value work and build the new paradigm that they and their kids deserve. Teachers, tutors, parents, and children all are interconnected in learning relationships and are part of an interdependent and ecological learning process. Duffy has set out the pathways not just to systemic change but to systemic wisdom and that is a spiritual route worth traveling. Ask Robert Pirsig!

Chapter Five

Wicked Problems and Loopy Solutions

> At the heart of our mental lives, there seems to be a striking contradiction—we seek out information and then act to destroy it. . . . We deny the truth to ourselves. We project on to others traits that are in fact true of ourselves—and then attack them!
>
> —Robert Trivers, 2011

Systems thinking operates optimally when applied to organizational confusion, assumptions, obfuscation, and ideology that those who tend to define school systems create and possibly depend on. It seeks out relevant information and tries to reveal what is true using fact, subjectivity, metaphor, and even metaphysics; whatever it takes to secure a better understanding of how a system works given what it is trying to achieve.

Books such as Robert Trivers's *The Folly of Fools* (2011), which turn the way we think about ourselves (if that is possible anymore) upside down, are a delight. They throw controversial light on the human condition and the way we tend to operate. For Trivers, self-deceit is biologically natural, a key survival mechanism passed on through memes and genes that offer biological edge. Such personal self-deception also seems to appease our psychological selves; it makes us feel better and justified, a form of self-aggrandizement that offers a rosier view of who we are.

Not only is our natural ability to distort and hide the truth a useful form of ego-protection, but such self-delusion also confers an advantage in all sorts of areas including reproduction and survival and, perhaps, a job for life! It is an illuminating theory. Perhaps our new-found emotional intelligence is just a mask, another means of asserting an advantage. If it is our prerogative (or more that of our unconscious) to manage our self-deluding ways of distorting truth to gain advantage, then we might expect to see evidence in organizational behaviors. We need not look far.

If we are so prone to self-deceit it is perfectly possible for much to remain hidden, to be assumed, and to remain apparently benign. We may do certain managerial tasks in school but offer a theoretical explanation that does not accurately match our action.

The previous chapter looked at delusion in part. In our schools, we continually try to build what we think are new *learning pathways*, but invariably we tend to recreate the system we already have; we might even make things even more dysfunctional while managing to convince ourselves that we have designed something new or at least fixed what was wrong. Trying to fix a broken system in the wrong way, using, say, classroom reform alone or new social programs and management techniques can actually create a more broken system or perpetuate the existing one. Our deluded beliefs are shown in our willingness to repeat again and again what does not work.

Systems thinking offers its own explanation of how such delusional behavior operates regarding organizations—one that may be more uncomfortably close to our deceitful biology than we might wish! Put bluntly, around education there is a huge job-creation program bent on maintaining the gravy train of the status quo and repeating past mistakes while claiming improvement. Systems thinking is able to side-step this blind-spot problem of willing self-deception, in part because it acts as an intuitive and detached observer unaffected by the system in question and so is better equipped to seek out any underpinning connectivity issues, the system's *fundamentals*, its basic design blueprint.

All of this, if accurate, can create a messy situation in which seemingly nothing ever gets properly resolved. If the linear system is to blame, there must be more evidence. The question is, how are we to think ourselves out of the wicked mess in which our schools appear to be?

SCHOOL AS A WICKED PROBLEM

Russell Ackoff (1970) described *messes* as exhibiting high levels of systems complexity that cannot be solved in isolation and that require holistic consideration and systems thinking as the best way out. He later spoke about *dissolving* seemingly intractable problems, redesigning the cultural environment rather than simply trying to *solve* problems superficially, only to create new ones elsewhere. In some ways, Ackoff was also highlighting two organizational concepts: loops and variation. In this chapter the focus is on single- and double-loop learning or (for me) closed-loop and open-loop thinking strategies.

The next stage up from a mess is a *wicked problem* caused by hyper-complexity, unpredictability, and changing social circumstances—the kind many schools face. Camillus (2008) set the scene this way:

Wicked problems often crop up when organizations have to face constant change or unprecedented challenges. They occur in a social context; the greater the disagreement among stakeholders, the more wicked the problem. In fact, it is the social complexity of wicked problems as much as their technical difficulties that make them tough to manage.

So we can rightly ask if schools are a wicked problem. They seem to defy reform, never change their fundamentals (basic system design), and even try to make photocopies of each other and call it improvement. It seems that schools in the United States fit the criteria all too well. Stephen Murgatroyd (2010) describes schools as "permanently failing organizations that never achieve the outcomes expected, being pulled in so many different directions by employers, parents, publishers, pressure groups, universities, government, health services, teachers, and unions." What we have, says Murgatroyd, are schools failing as organizations run by a "demoralized profession that has become little more than an army of target-obsessed box tickers."

Murgatroyd is not alone in thinking this way, but he believes that teachers hold the key to change. He might argue that most educational change strategies in other more successful jurisdictions entail a high degree of consultation and teacher involvement, so one challenge, one part of any solution, rests in empowering our teachers to be more of the transforming people they were meant to be. What we have is an endless promotion of wild and unproven theorizing in teaching, managing, and leading followed by a nasty habit of directly blaming teachers and schools when things do not pan out as expected. We need to explore more precisely why this is and how it might be linked to the old industrial linear model.

Part of the reason for this is research. Almost all school research is based on the acceptance of the horizontal system as organizationally benign and *normal*, the way schools are and have always been. Why should their linear nature be of the slightest interest? When schools apply the research conclusions or the new program, the fact is that the existing organizational fundamentals continue unchanged and unchallenged. The proposal here is that this is what causes the intended reform to fail or be compromised. The school is then blamed for its failure of fidelity. We need to understand why this is. What is it that appears to be happening?

UNDERSTANDING LEARNING LOOPS

Chris Argyris and Donald Schön (1978), a psychologist and a philosopher, are concerned with organizational learning. They tell us that we are all guided by mental maps, which we learn and develop over time. These govern our managerial actions and tell us the best action to take, how best to plan and implement strategies, and how to subsequently review what we have done. Did it work or not, and why? These mental maps are powerful influences on behavior and tend to be our first resort. The problem is that our mental maps appear to have a delusionary quality. The actions taken are invariably justified as being part of a theoretical underpinning, which, according to Argyris and Schön, rarely tally. So what managers do and how they explain the theory behind what they do are two different things. There is a split.

Part of the reason for this is that in a high procedural and rule-bound organization like a school the concern is always to do the *right thing* as opposed to *doing what is right*. Doing the right thing is built into the mental map and may well win you promotion, part of our deceitful or delusional self perhaps. The manager's concern is to work within the accepted and normal parameters of the organization and not to deviate too far. If something goes wrong and the mental map gives what some call a bum steer, an alternative strategy or variation is always at hand. All of these actions are single-loop learning in nature. They use only those strategies available and follow the rules keeping well within the organization's governing variables.

This helps explain why schools self-perpetuate variations on a theme, often returning to the first variation, the single-loop circularity. In this way the theoretical explanation never quite matches the action taken. This mismatch between mental maps that govern actions and theoretical intentions and explanations makes the school susceptible to odd behaviors when it comes to reform. What politicians and policy makers intend is likely to be absorbed into mental maps as an interpretation. Even vocabulary can be confusing. Words such as *entitlement* and phrases such as *broad and balanced curriculum* or slogans such as *No child left behind* lack clarity and meaning. The result is that the school actually changes only marginally. That is not to say things do not get better. They sometimes do.

Schools use all the techniques at their disposal to improve. They often believe that they are working in a stressful maelstrom of incessant organizational flux, but the fact is that there is no organizational change, just stasis. But all that is happening is a frustrated change to techniques; enigma variations on a theme justified by theory that does not hold.

Argyris and Schön (1978) identified a different approach to the way organizational detection and correction of errors is handled, namely double-loop learning.

> Double-loop learning occurs when error is detected and corrected in ways that involve the modification of an organization's underlying norms, policies and objectives.

In effect this literally means changes to the system fundamentals. Rather than follow the existing norms, policies, and objectives of schools, why not question the underpinning learning system? But therein is the problem. Schools may think that this is what they are doing all the time, an ongoing task. The fact is that school managers and leaders are far too close to the system that handed out the mental maps, which enable every person in the country to understand fairly precisely how schools operate. What they cannot possibly see is that every action, every obstacle, everything they do is culturally driven not by values but by linear design. And this is totally ignored as being in any way problematic.

In some ways, difficult problems can be approached using either method, but each will have a different resolution and different consequences. When applied to schools, loop theory makes a great deal of sense and offers helpful insights into creating a systems thinking school, an organization that is self-learning. But to get there requires rewriting mental maps, and such unlearning presents a huge training challenge for many. In turn this also means understanding how the linear industrial design operates at such a subtle and insidious level to keep things the same. We need to return to the original industrial school blueprint passed down over time.

The industrial school comprises a linear input-output model. To a large degree, its design mimicked the penchant for efficient scientific method and sought to prepare young people to take their place in an industrialized world as workers capable of acting on instructions from above. Its working fundamentals and assumptions have changed little over many decades despite rapidly changing times. Students enter school, receive instruction, are sorted and batched, and should then exit school with sufficient knowledge to take their appropriate place in the world outside. It is the design of this basic model that should be of interest to school managers.

On entry to a secondary school, the child quickly ends up in a classroom having received either minimal induction or no preparation whatsoever. The school believes and assumes that the classroom is the key place where the magic happens, where learning relationships form and learning occurs. The industrial public school model existed to deliver instruction as efficiently as possible with a fairly distinctive separation between teacher and learner, and teacher and home. What is really distinctive about this model is not so much its efficiency but its simplicity—a theme we shall return to.

In its basic form, it is a model designed to deliver information and sufficient skill needed to handle such information. Any information delivery system is invariably formal and one way. Feedback is not really required, nor within such a system is it easily usable even if it were available. In effect, it comprises a straightforward, single-loop teaching organization, and this is hugely limiting.

Should there be any deviation from normal working practices, the school's thermostatic control raises or lowers the heat to ensure normal working is resumed without further ado. There would be little reason to involve parents who at best remain on the receiving end of the school's one-way information system. Compliancy was the culture of the day (despite the occasional riot) and in many ways this remains the case. However, it is not the compliancy, coercion, and control (the 3 Cs) or the 3 Rs that are the industrial schools' most distinctive features; such schools were not beyond innovation. It is its inherent linearity, and these operational fundamentals have changed not one jot over the years.

THE BASIC INDUSTRIAL PROCESS

To change the nature or systemically redesign how a system works requires that we at least understand it as an operational process: in particular, we need to come to terms with how and why the linear model throws up distortions and manages to ensure that it is protected in space and time from any double-loop interference. This includes its distortional effect on almost all research projects that seek to analyze it and instigate reformational ideas to change it. Without such an understanding, successful systemic change is unlikely.

The industrial and linear school model is a simple input-output mechanism. It receives raw materials from numerous suppliers at the input end (upstream). It processes the raw materials by sifting and sorting them into different batches by type, using a crude grading system. These are labeled and delivered to customers in the marketplace according to demand. Any broken or ungraded units may be unemployable and must survive as best they can.

This system has not really changed, but the world beyond the school certainly has. Downstream, the marketplace is unhappy with the quality of goods leaving the factory. Upstream, family suppliers feel under pressure and worried. They have become choosier about where the raw material they produce is best processed, have started to regard themselves as the true customers, and even believe they should have an input into the grading process.

And of course, the raw material they supply is not what it was. It has become far more difficult and variable and this is making it difficult to process. This is not helped by a processing system split into three completely different and disconnected factory plants. Not only does the raw material not travel well between these sections, but the sections themselves are also run by completely different management people. Mistakes and process delays in the upstream junior and middle plants necessitate massive repeat work in the secondary plants. As a result, almost eight thousand units, called dropouts, disappear from the secondary factory each day without being properly finished. Everyone is unhappy and all attempts to arrest the situation seem to fail despite best intentions.

And now for one of the many space and time differences between the way the system is and the way we interpret or see the system. Research tells us many things, except the things we need to know in order to redesign the process. Class size, we are told is not the problem, extending time on task does not seem to do the trick; so pretty soon we are left looking at the teacher in the classroom who has now gone into hiding and is unavailable for comment. We are in the world of delusion.

The industrial model is all about managing large numbers of people. Efficiency was always the watchword: low cost, high output, 100 percent of goods processed. But now the system has become inefficient and wasteful of its precious raw material. Too many young people leave unfit for employment in the labor market. Add these to those who drop out and the numbers start to look very bad indeed, and it is the numbers that hold the clue to change. If class sizes do not affect output performance, we need not worry about the numbers, surely, but this would be a space and time separation mistake.

Increases to input variation in terms of behavior, attitude, language acumen, incentive, culture, home environment, and so on comprise the increasingly complex challenge for schools. What is of critical importance is not class size, but it is the system's ability to adapt accordingly to the increasingly individual nature of the large numbers being handled, given the new demands of customers. So much so that the students themselves have become customers. These new drivers should have changed the internal operational workings but this has not happened in any substantive way.

When we accept that class size is not an issue, everyone is left standing looking puzzled at what is. This results in a frenzy of single-loop activity that fails to impact on quality output. Numbers and the way they are handled is the issue. What the school should realize is that to be a service provider in such an important and delicate area requires an individualized and more bespoke approach. We should have seen the school as an organization developing internally in a way where service and communication becomes de rigueur (i.e., everyone provides and receives services and this means a massive increase in information traffic and changes to support services but none of this has happened as it should).

None of this is the fault of schools or teachers, but it is a fault. The class size business and research interpretations threw us. Research into schools invariably looks at single-loop activity and single-loop thinking; what else is there to see? The mental maps remain firmly in place, and that means an unlearning problem!

In particular, attention must be called to the relationship between parents and teachers. As a design feature, this relationship was never thought necessary and so was never considered as an important feature, and was not built into the original design. Despite a huge variety of methods, practices, and claims to the contrary, this separation remains today and is explored in more detail later. Parent partnership is all but non-existent in all schools, despite myriad models trying to suggest otherwise, and this absence and the inadequacy of existing practice is causing severe social difficulties for families and young people. The same might be said of teacher and student learning relationships.

There remains a space and time gap between all players caused directly by the linear nature of the underlying structure. The school has been unable to move from a batch system to a more personalized one; it is a numbers problem and a big quality control issue. Any resolution requires that the school has to make changes deep within its structure, double-loop. The linear system has become dangerous, damaging, and dysfunctional and has to change.

When a child enters the classroom today, that child may easily be taught by a dozen or so different teachers in a week and probably many more different teachers in the school year. There are at least three different school phases to navigate, each requiring a fresh start with different teachers. Throughout his or her schooling, the child may be taught by a hundred or more different teachers. Conversely, a teacher may teach a hundred or more different students in a week. This adds risk to learning because of the inability or delays involved in creating (personalized) learning relationships of any meaning conducive to good child development and learning.

The original model was never created to be parent friendly or even *friendly*! Sending reports home was minimal, communicating with parents even rarer if at all. Besides, how could there possibly be such a working relationship? Teachers still have to get to know vast numbers of students so the chances of learning relationships forming, let alone being considered as in any way important for learning, remains low and largely fortuitous. The fact that there are any learning relationships worthy of the name is a reflection of our outstanding teachers, not the system in play.

Information tends to be trapped inside classrooms, rarely escaping, and this too has not changed. It has become a frustration that the system that has endured has been unable to evolve in a way whereby all significant adults, parents, and staff can participate fully in not only supporting learning but also in being part of the operational learning and support process. This means that schools, try as they might, continue to operate using limited information and ever-repeating single-loop learning strategies confined to classrooms—a system entirely reliant on teacher brilliance and, therefore, largely a matter of serendipity.

The system as it stands simply does not have a means whereby school and home are able to form an effective learning alliance with each other and the child. This means that schools operate with less contextual knowledge and limited socio-psychological knowledge (held by parents), and this tends to dampen any ecological fit and causes the school to seek alternative substitute strategies—but always ways that are single-loop learning in essence. Even if each of a child's teachers were fully briefed on each of the hundred children they might be teaching in a given week, such information overload could prove too overwhelming to contemplate and use. Put simply, in the existing industrial model, learning relationships take considerable time to form and such time lags are now unacceptably risky and expensive (waste). Compliance remains the preferred way.

OF LOOPS AND MENTAL MAPS

Single-loop learning tends to keep the system's governing variables and actions within the realm of how the system normally operates, and this prevents adaptation and defies attempts at substantive change. So although we now have myriad different schools, we have no real transformation. In a private school, things are not really any better despite high graduation rates. Making a system appear to work does not make it right. Here, parents purchase compliance, which is included in the deal; this enables teaching to occur, but in such schools lower class sizes are important. Although class sizes may make no noticeable difference to outcomes, they make a significant difference to factors such as personal attention, feeling valued, feeling part of an organization that truly cares, and being known rather than being anonymous as so many students can choose to be.

All of this explains much about the failure of reform and its single-loop ways. Double-loop learning is concerned with questioning knowledge fundamentals; hence it requires a systems thinking approach that is not phased by space and time separation. Not only does double-loop learning question assumptions and fundamentals, but it is also a more creative way of seeking cultural and holistic solutions to problems and especially wicked ones.

Strangely, there is also a spiritual dimension to double-loop learning. Its concern with values, quality, and purpose as design guidelines means it is also much more aligned to *goodness* both as an end goal and as a way of proceeding. In many respects, double-loop learning combines psychology and philosophy with organizational design and this make such learning more systems thinking in essence. The system is the enabling organization that allows people to work at their best or as Deming so aptly put it, *with joy*. The challenge is to make work work, to enable all parties to function at their best with a shared mental map of how the entire system works together, rather than each carrying their own secret map.

Dominant single-loop learning works well in simple systems. Nobody gets too upset! Nothing much changes and remedies can usually be easily incorporated. Schools started out as simple systems and single-loop strategies were more than sufficient. However, changing environmental conditions, technological change, and increased social and learning complexity are all impacting on the demand side to create the wicked problem we have. Today, schools are still far too simple as systems and this is why, paradoxically, they can so easily drown in any new complexities. Their single-loop learning ways prevent their self-emergence and evolution as learning organizations. The simple thermostatic control of single-loop learning can no longer handle the environmental and ecological demand. If schools are to be the butterflies we need them to be, cracking the hard shell of the single-loop chrysalis is essential and this means redesigning for systemic change.

The constant changes and tinkering to the peripheral parts simply causes oscillation and a system forever trying to correct itself; as Deming (1994) said, "The prevailing style of management must undergo transformation. A system cannot understand itself. The transformation requires a view from outside." In part this is because school managers cannot *see* what is needed in such a closed system. They are far too close to it and are trained *not* to look at organizational structures (seemingly beyond their remit) but to look at people operators because in *Schoolworld* it is people, not systems, that appear to be the cause of mess-ups. School managers geared to single-loop fixes for double-loop problems, makes them part of the expensive waste and flow problem.

Double-loop learning, according to Usher and Bryant (1989) goes to the root of the system's process and "involves questioning the role of the framing and learning systems which underlie actual goals and strategies." In a school, this means looking at the totality of the learning process, at accepted fundamentals, patterns, and assumptions. Mark Smith's (2001) overview of the work of Chris Agyris is a systems thinking gem for those interested.

The single-loop question posed by Adam Kahane (2004) asks, "Are we doing things right?" The double-loop (the interconnected and information-rich loop or open-loop) asks the question, "Are we doing the right things?" Only by unlearning *doing things right* can schools start to *do the right things* and so be rescued from the delusion foisted on them by traditional and industrial school management theory. Schools simply need to be put back in touch with more of themselves, their absent purpose, their quest for quality, and their values. This means looking again at what constitutes a quality learning relationship.

Chapter Six

Applying Single-Loop Strategies to Double-Loop Problems

It is the wise manager who learns to manage value, not cost. No back office, no targets, no activity management, but instead a thorough understanding of citizen demand and staff with the wherewithal to deal with it.

—John Seddon, 2013

There is a problem to be faced by the systems thinking school and it involves managing complexity. Richard Chase (1978) wrote about the failure of service sector organizations, which included schools, to adopt similar technocratic systems as manufacturing. He proposed a back-office solution: the less direct contact the customer (parent) has with the service system (teachers), the greater the potential of the system to operate at peak efficiency—precisely the opposite in many respects, of the proposals in this book. Conversely, where the direct customer contact is great, the less potential exists to achieve high levels of service efficiency. In such a scenario, the role of the manager is to get people working hard and this means preventing customers from interrupting their work.

The challenge to any systems thinking school, therefore, is how to connect the school and the parent to ensure an ongoing double-loop learning conversation. In schools, managers are convinced that every moment in the day has to be accounted for and maximally used. In many schools, as demand for more complex services (special needs, gifted and talented, inclusion, new pro-social programs, etc.) increases, so the schools' back offices have grown to deal with demand, allowing teachers to teach. In turn, this has increased management, organizational complexity, and costs. In the United Kingdom this is called *workforce reform* and has been erroneously labeled as one of seven ill-conceived *learning gateways*.

For many, school provides an opportunity that is akin to drinking at the last-chance saloon and parents have increasingly and rightly felt the need for more involvement in such an important process, especially so as the gap in US society between the haves and have nots, rich and poor, healthy and unhealthy, in work and not in work, increases. School remains a slim life chance for many. Chase (1978) recommended a simple solution for managing customer demand: front offices should be set up where customers (parents) could make contact with the service provider (school) and the customer's requirements then sent to the back office for processing.

Most schools have such systems in place but such a simple fix is not quite what it seems. Arguably, the industrial model had already decoupled parent customers from teacher service provision so any back-office access via a front-office portal, although a step in the right direction, can only realize the separation that already exists. The rich communication link between home and school and child and teacher on which much double-loop learning depends, remains largely absent and is slow to form if it forms at all. This places the teacher, parent, and child in potential jeopardy in terms of learning support and personal development.

The absence, inherited through the industrial linear model, of this key home-school-child relationship continues to undermine the effectiveness of schools and learning as a complete operational process. There is a failure to appreciate the sophisticated nature of parent, teacher, and student demand and how all three should be inextricably linked. Somehow, a systems thinking school has to ensure that these fundamental interconnections are in place and able to inform the learning support job. Otherwise, there can be no *thorough understanding* in John Seddon's terms, or indeed the *wherewithal to deal with it*.

The questions and solutions Chase (2010) posed in a later review do little to help. Although recognizing that schools are classified as high in terms of the quality contact needed between customer and service provider, the solutions for schools fall short of a working partnership. They still seem to see customers as somehow problematic and having to be separately managed albeit in new ways using virtual technology, appointment systems, or by ensuring that *people*-type people work closest to them in the front office. All of this is precisely what schools do and although it is a step in the direction of a double-loop conversation with home it tends toward an approach used after a problem has arisen. This makes such an option an add-on for customers to access rather than an integrated communication system for all designed to prevent negative demand arising from system failure.

If parents are seen as end users of an information system rather than as integral partners in an interconnected learning organization, we can expect changes in technique (single-loop) rather than substance (double-loop). One of these might be to simplify and reduce information home to avoid negative demands (complaints and inquiries) coming back and disrupting services! We have to find a way of connecting the main caregivers with schools and young people as an implicit part of the learning process. That design change has to be double-loop, a change to the system's fundamentals.

The reality is that our industrial schools now have to deal with increasing complexity. Bullying is as much virtual as direct, drug experimentation is high, warning signs of reprisals are easy to miss, mental illness is on the increase, and so the list goes on. There may even be less compassion just as there is less well-being. One academic advised that the next time we read about a US boy going to school and shooting his fellow students, ask where he learned such problem-solving skills. He was talking about the power of TV and films. All of these matters matter and schools are in the front line for not only managing the fall out, but also for prevention, and the current means are insufficient.

A systems thinking school has to maximize a sense of belonging and compassion, and this means working with parents as never before. This can only be done when we stop seeing management in the narrow way our restricted single-loop learning allows. Any contact with a school tends to start with the front office (point of customer contact), which then places a request to the big back office (processes hidden from the customer's view). Not only does this funneling of information restrict flow, but it can also cause overload in both front and back offices.

In the back office, requests can be delayed, lost, misinterpreted, and mistakes made in a place where the view of the customer is so much less compassionate than that of the front office, being estranged as it is in space and time. Any single-loop learning initiative may at its best improve information, but the concurrent downside remains the absence of communication, which is a two-way process. This is an unaffordable omission from any systems thinking organization and especially one in the service sector school where information is critical to intervention, support, and learning.

THE DOUBLE-LOOP WAY FORWARD

The double-loop learning initiative involves changing the school's organizational culture rather than self-perpetuating the problem. The real answer is not the large institutional back-office expansion accessed via a single front-office portal of some kind (single-loop learning solution). What is actually needed are multiple front offices in a single school that are capable of not only managing the complex demands of parents, teachers, and young people, but also a system capable of predicting the demands most likely to bring increases of service quality throughout the system. Such a system has to be hyper-responsive and capable of rapid intervention.

The reality is that most schools already have these front offices (home groups), but none are operationally effective, and many have a negative learning effect. The linear culture renders them moribund as an effective means of delivering high-quality services by stifling communication rather than enhancing it. Only by changing horizontal tutor groups and home groups to mixed-age VT can the system spark into life; what it was meant to be. This book simply explains how this is done and how the back office adjusts to suit and serve the multi-nodal front-office access points.

PLUS ÇA CHANGE: PARENT PARTNERSHIP

In schools, teachers are constantly trying to improve their techniques and develop more effective protocols; reformers are trying to implement new programs; researchers are trying to get a handle on our penchant for repetition, and parents are trying to get a foot in the door. All tend toward single-loop learning approaches, whereby the fundamentals of school remain intact to the frustration of systemic changers and romantic liberals.

At the periphery of the linear, industrial school, parents are beginning to organize themselves, and we need to understand how the system in play creates a situation whereby, for all of their efforts, they are more likely to end up talking among themselves than with the school!

Two examples relating to parent partnership are described below. The first reveals tensions and undesirable outcomes when there is a lack of understanding and appreciation of home-school partnership when one system (school) is unable to respond to another (home) to form an expanded learning system. The second is a classic approach to reform that reveals the degree to which schools are erroneously perceived as simple single-loop operations to which fixes can easily be added. Both are examples of single-loop learning trying to resolve a double-loop problem. The purpose is to show that linear systems cannot flex and are actually made more complex by each approach and, therefore, destined to fail.

Each single-loop solution further distorts the system it seeks to correct and makes it even more intransigent to real change. The inevitable result is reduced flow, increased waste, back-office expansion, and process damage that does more harm than good while wrongly indicating that the detected problem (improved partnership) has been resolved. Of course, when the fix fails, someone is to blame and so the cycle re-starts. Almost any kind of school reform-type strategy can be chosen given that most are single-loop applications.

Parent Partnership Part 1: Flawed Implementation

The involvement of parents in the learning process is regarded as critical in creating a systems thinking school. But, as Deming always asked, by what method? Home-school partnership is a misunderstood and long-standing problem. Not one secondary school in the hundreds with which I have worked has come close to understanding or resolving this challenge. They have assumed that their relationship with parent customers was good, in line with normal practice, and that practice accurately encapsulated values.

Parent partnership certainly needs to be tackled given that our kids need stability and affirmation, but schools cannot resolve the problem in the way parents want given the limitations of linear style management and, therefore, the knowledge they have. When such tired management methodologies grow moribund, the school is exposed to external reform edicts that lack school ownership and coherence. *Authorities* soon step in to devise school policy and best practice. So what could possibly go wrong? Answer: the method!

There is near-universal agreement for improvements in partnership between school and home, and the National Alliance for Secondary Education and Transition (NASET) based at the University of Minnesota (2010) has set out some of the vast body of research that supports this. In the United States, Joyce Epstein and colleagues (1997) proposed six national standards for parental involvement and partnership.

This partnership framework between school and home is as follows:

- Communicating: effective communication between home and school.
- Parenting: skills promoted and supported.
- Volunteering: parental involvement in school encouraged and facilitated.
- Home learning.
- School decision making: parental participation.
- Collaboration with community: community used as a resource to strengthen schools, families, and learning.

This is as good a description of parent partnership as we are likely to get, and it nails the important areas. Before schools say that they already do these things or complain that they already have a day job, we should be at least able to agree that these are all desirables. These are well-thought-out, rational, admirable, well-researched, and evidence-based goals; these are all activities that can help to improve learning, teaching, and even parenting. So, what is the problem? The problem lies in how, if at all, this brings about cultural system change. The framework describes facets of double-loop learning, and this requires fundamental changes to the way the organization operates.

Unfortunately, the linear nature of the school's structure only allows single-loop learning solutions, and this is likely to lead to unforeseen system distortions that result in undesirable consequences. In essence, communication and partnership is the stuff of double-loop learning, but schools are largely single-loop operations in their linear form. This false reality of how schools are perceived as learning organizations (our mental maps) make it almost impossible for players to judge whether any final partnership implementation scheme by the school is successful or not!

The process of implementation is flawed from the outset. It begins with the school's (not the parents') inability to embrace the home subsystem as an integral part of the child's learning process, to complete a full learning system. There is a good reason for this: the linear school model places a huge but unrecognized limit on the ability of the school to communicate effectively with families given its back-office preference. This deep design flaw is actually hidden from both schools and parents. It is another irresolvable facet of the wicked problem that is the school as an organization.

The result is to view the home-school partnership as a superficial organizational problem rather than a cultural one and to deem appropriate, single-loop fixes with their inadequate communication and information flow. In effect, we end up with a repair job when more substantive organizational change is needed. Eventually parents or districts get involved, self-organize, and work with or around the school to provide a solution. Like an iceberg, the real problem as to why parents are not properly involved in their child's learning and are actively distanced from it, lies deep in the flawed system fundamentals of the horizontal structure. The industrial nature of school was never designed with parents in mind, so the double interconnective loop that the framework suggests, is simply absent. The real solution, vertical organization, and multiple personal front offices, remains hidden.

The *standards* then take on a life of their own, oblivious to the real challenges within the industrial design. The standards comprise values and principles but simply sticking to these is likely to be organizationally brushed aside or assumed by the school. To prevent this there is a move from values to actions and strategies, from double- to single-loop learning and implementation methodologies. Each standard is broken down into several criteria and so management complexity increases almost as an imposition, albeit a friendly one.

The new framework is then implanted on top of the existing broken (linear) school system framework. Schools tick-box the criteria and set aside back-office staff and time to manage the new standards and their many derivatives. Evaluations are needed, targets set and measured, agreements drawn up, meetings arranged, records kept, and activity and costs increase. But little actually changes at any fundamental cultural level—except that the school has to work significantly harder in this area at a cost to other areas for spurious benefit!

Ros Kanter (1989) offered an excellent corporate description on the nature of partnership, whereas Charles Handy (1995) offers us the idea of the Chinese contract. The former sets out essential partnership requirements, and the latter seeks to avoid the social and economic cost of compelling compliance. While working in the East, Handy began to write down the contractual nature of an agreement but was interrupted by his negotiating partner. "In my culture," he went on, "a good agreement is self enforcing because both parties go away smiling and are happy to see that the other is smiling." Handy noted the cultural change where negotiation was about finding the best way forward for both parties.

The inflexibility of linear organization desires such an approach but acts to prevent any practical and workable application. Indeed, the relationship between school and home can even deteriorate when compliance, as opposed to joint benefit, gets in the way of values: this is especially so if schools see more work and accountability coming their way: smiles through gritted teeth! The parents think they have got what they want but have actually created a bastardized and bureaucratized version of what is needed and what was intended: yet another reform change blind-sided on a school. What can actually be created is a huge amount of waste and the high potential for negative demand—the very things that block flow and prevent the value work.

Any small gains made are pyrrhic and can actually make the wicked problem worse rather than better. But people (the active parents in particular) are convinced that the new fix is the answer. It is a case, as Ackoff suggested in his Villanova speech (1999), of doing the *right things* (trying to improve home-school partnership) *wronger*. The problem with the schools we have is in part their lack of an interconnected communication system within the school capable of enhancing learning as a process that extends way beyond the classroom to parents and back again, a complete double- or open-learning loop. Back-office approaches ensure schools operate information systems and not the communication networks all parties (i.e., home, school, students) actually need, and as such we end up with incompatible partners.

Similarly, as soon as the principles and values are reduced to single-loop learning strategies, it becomes a case of *plus ça change plus c'est la même chose*: the more things change, the more they stay the same. At best, an imposed single-loop implant may increase frequency of information, more e-mails perhaps, but it is the way information is used qualitatively in the complete learning process that is important. This cannot be achieved using single-loop learning information strategies alone. The fundamentals of schools are not qualitatively changed by such add-ons and can even become more culturally and defensibly entrenched by the actions taken.

This build-a-separate-add-on-system approach so universally adopted can actually undermine the important role of parenting, and does. No matter what standards are set, they will always lead to system distortions and are more likely to create negative demand. Even decision making (the fifth standard in the Minnesota framework) can simply act to endorse and extend *what is* (doing things right) rather than changing *what's necessary* (doing the right things). The problem of a malfunctioning system is that it invites and creates wrong fixes that are likely to cause other knock-on malfunctioning problems, increasing the space and time distance between cause and effect.

All of these plausible and well-intentioned parent partnership matters can erroneously become *standards* (fixes) in the absence of a workable whole-school learning process able to embrace parents and build learning relationships throughout. Standards bring with them old ideas such as targets, accountabilities, reviews, policies, practices, tick-sheets, more work, and all of this can so easily constitute highly expensive waste. Imagine the time and implementation costs in meetings, paperwork, administration, and checking and all with no real change to fundamentals.

The irony is that parents will sense an improvement but at a huge cost. The reality is that things will get worse by entrenching the wrong method, sapping energy from the school rather than invigorating flow and learning. Because the school has no complete double-or open-loop learning process involving parents as an integral process part, a mini-monster system is created to provide an alternative. Instead of *Breakfast at Tiffany's* we end up with an uneasy marriage between two seemingly incongruous and flawed partners, both sticking around because of the kids and both secretly hankering after a divorce. This is not good for kids and no one gets to keep the cat!

Instead of being process-coherent and interconnected, parent partnership becomes learning-process deficient, supporting more bad practices than good. Reality gets distorted, the paradox is not seen and the system not only fails to change, but also gets wickeder and wronger. Standards tend to define a system's techniques as Usher and Bryant (1989) suggest, when redesign and transformation are needed, while targets always lead to distorted outcomes.

So what is the elegant double-loop solution? A systems thinking school with a VT communication arrangement is dependent on families as an integral learning partnership that requires no breakdown into separate entities and standards. Quality is built into the complete learning process, making the need for such standards an oddity. Vertical systems act to enhance quality, create time and space to suit, but all of this has to be systems thinking learned. All is explained as we build the systems thinking school. At the moment, the task is to look at schools and gain the knowledge needed to ensure that the Borg are unable to operate as they do.

Parent Partnership Part 2: The Parent Partnership Toolbox

Schools have at best adopted a piecemeal approach to parent partnership. At the secondary level, they simply miss the point about partnership principles and purpose and the nature of what constitutes the communication needed within a full operational learning process. In the case of year-based or grade systems (linear), parent partnership can never work properly because the learning function involving formative and summative assessments of which it is part can never be completed. (A whole chapter is devoted to this important process later.)

The National College for Leadership of Schools and Children's Services (NCSL) website posted a document designed to help schools improve parental engagement: *Leading and Developing Parental Engagement—A Tool to Help You Audit and Improve Your Practice* (NCSL 2011). This is just what schools like to see: a research-based rationale (good) translated into a better way forward (disaster) by those who erroneously perceive school structures as benign. It is another single-loop attempt at resolving a double-loop design fault. The previous model was top-down, this one is bottom-up, but sensible schools will reject it anyway.

First, schools are required to read an earlier and longer research document, which basically says that parental involvement is useful in many ways and for many reasons. OK, schools probably get that. What schools are then given is a set of complicated toolbox instructions about the *three-phase approach* to improving parent partnership. Part of this requires schools to absorb previous research on parent partnership to access the toolbox, a sort of toolbox to open a toolbox. School leaders are then invited to go through the toolbox document first and then the whole school, itself a big task, resulting in an immediate breakdown in fidelity.

Schools are then presented with the *5-ways tool* and from this point on, matters get very complex indeed. After reading the 2008 background report, trying to comprehend the instructions to open the toolbox, and then mentally trying to remember the numerous issues required to navigate the *5–ways tool*, schools eventually arrive at the audit proper. Audits are big in education: they tell you nothing and are single-loop in essence but are seen as covering all compliancy bases. The audit section requires schools to complete a further 107 different comment boxes.

By the time we get to the last tool in this box of unpleasant tricks, *the prioritization matrix tool*, most should realize that this toolbox approach to a simple communication issue will not work.

Toolboxes like this can never replace knowledge; neither do they create the right methodology for progress, and in particular, substantive change. What should take a systems thinking school five minutes to resolve is presented as a task of Kafkaesque proportions devoid of any conception of a valid and doable operational process. Schools foolish enough to engage with this kind of approach will conclude that parent partnership is hugely complex, probably impossible to manage, and not worth the effort.

As ever, the title is misleading and silly, yet this is not untypical of the improvement and reform paraphernalia that surrounds our schools and which many schools buy into as good management and leadership practice. Suffice it to say, a systems thinking school builds parent partnership into the learning process with a more harmonious and coherent ease and at no cost! But that requires a little redesign and not buying into distortions that add to our tendency for managerial self-delusion.

The reason schools are open to toolbox-style approach rests entirely with their linear form. Having seen almost every conceivable variation of parent partnership in year-based schools, there has not been one that comes close to matching the six standards originally set out by Epstein and colleagues (1997). To build parent partnership *in* rather than *add it on* requires that the school is able to understand how the linear system is limiting and how to culturally put things right.

And then comes the tricky part. The horizontal tutoring system has to be *dismantled and replaced by a vertical system. Only then* can the affect relationships kick-in and be integrated into the operational learning process of the school, so completing the assessment for the learning (AFL) cycle that involves parents and students. It all comes down to the principles of time management and the restoration of values that VT demands on behalf of all customers, internal and external.

Trying to change schools from outside to in is almost impossible without unlearning much that comprises traditional school management. This requires systems thinking know-how and a better approach to training school managers. Neither is there an easy way forward for schools to culturally redesign themselves from inside to out, although an approach recommended by Charles Reigeluth (2006) holds possibilities. Reigeluth calls this "leveraged emergent design." An emergent process, as the title suggests, requires school leaders and others to discover those design changes most likely to start a domino effect that can lead to holistic change by impacting on all system parts.

Such a model allows the school as an organization to evolve and re-culture at a fast rate without the drama of a complete and instant makeover and offers the possibility of greater ownership. This book promotes an organizational change from the blocked single-learning loops of a horizontal system to the double, open feedback, and interconnected communication loops of a vertically managed systems thinking school as our best *emergent* bet.

The domino effect is attractive: once home groups transform from being same-age to all-age constituencies, itself a change driven by customer care values, it causes all other parts to adapt accordingly. This is because this first structural design change creates front offices throughout the school, opening the door to full internal and external interconnectivity; a kind of hyperactive evolutionary effect that allows the system to rebuild itself in a joined, open-loop, and systems thinking way.

Jeff Dooley (1995) suggested a clever and classic motto for any systems intervention: *If it's not fixed, don't break it.* The corollary is this: if someone has tried to fix an organizational fault and believes that it has cured the problem, then there is a real problem; so the best thing to do is break it all up and start again. In schools, there is conflict and distortion regarding values that loop theory can inform and perhaps we are too hard on the school reformer. Dooley describes this distortion effect and the nature of self-delusion elegantly:

> A result of this disconnect between our espoused values and the values we enact is that we may, upon making an error, act to protect ourselves from embarrassment or threat by distorting or covering-up key information about the error. This usually saves us, but it has the unfortunate consequence of also inhibiting just the kind of organizational learning that would be required to examine the conditions that gave rise to the error in the first place. We have acted in a way that has probably hurt the organization, yet we don't usually think of ourselves as saboteurs; we simply do what seems to make sense given the dilemmas of organizational life.

Systems cannot *self-improve* unless they are *self-aware* and have a clear purpose and link to society and the world at large. Those who come in bent on improvement are likely to walk straight past the fundamental design issue causing the problem and then contribute to the perceived problem by trying to repair using single-loop learning alone. They will be like aid agencies entering a disaster zone and creating more harm than good by failing to see what is needed, what works, and how the system aligns to its environment and local context—what people need as opposed to what we insist they have.

The key attribute of a (school) leader is to be able to listen to the wisdom of the system (Meadows 2009). This requires a little systems thinking know-how. Otherwise, schools will pass on as much inherited bad practice as good, their ignorance of which reflects highly theoretical training options, an acceptance of received system assumptions, and a misleading leadership rationale—all of which are single-loop in essence. There is another insidious effect. Without real purpose and method, schools are exposed to the theoretical excesses of reformers, fixers, and peddlers who target the classroom and the teacher as the weak point in the system. It is this very targeting that makes schools weak and this targeting is *of* the system.

A friend sent me a cartoon. A teacher is sitting behind a desk in a large open field. Nearby is a large and tall tree. In front of the teacher, the class lines up facing the teacher. It is an unusual class. It includes a bird, a goldfish in a bowl, an elephant, a monkey, a giraffe, a seal, a lion, and a host of other creatures.

"Right," says the teacher, "I want this test to be as fair as possible. You have one hour starting now to complete the test. Climb that tree!"

Chapter Seven

Reform and Variation as Wicked Problems

With expected variation improvement is secured by improving the process or system. With unexpected variation management will seek to identify the cause of the instability. It is a common costly mistake to fail to differentiate between these two types of variation.

—W. Edwards Deming, 1994

In practice, data does not amount to a hill of beans unless it is accessible and able to teach us something useful about system improvement. When school experts talk about variation, they often get heavily into data charts and statistics. More simply, an unusual downward spike in a student's performance output, something that was not predicted, usually has a *special cause*. The student may have been unwell. If the whole class is underperforming there may have been a teacher change that month. Spot the variation, account for it, fix the problem, and return the system to its predictable, stable self. This is called *special cause variation*. This type of variation is often unpredictable but can usually be put right when noticed.

When unusual things happen in an organization (an unexpected variation), positive or negative, managers rightly ask questions. They try and find out what it was that worked, or more likely, did not work, and they decide a course of action accordingly. But much of that action is single-loop, changes to technique or changes at a fairly superficial level of practice that some call *tampering*. In schools, managers tend to deal entirely with this type of special cause variation and this is what teachers expect of them. In most cases, the aim is to ensure that the unexpected event does not reoccur.

However, if school output variations continue to fluctuate there comes a time when the methods used by managers seem to fail. The cause appears to be beyond the managerial capability of the organization and can no longer be fixed. People rightly look at complex social conditions, social well-being, poverty, and aspirations, all of which can affect school performance detrimentally. But eventually, the finger starts to point to the classroom and at the teacher and sparks a whole debate about school quality, relevance, and purpose. When things keep going wrong at work, our tendency is to blame those that operate or work in the system, a people quality problem.

W. Edwards Deming (1986) thought otherwise. He estimated that around 94 percent of variation has its origins elsewhere, with the system itself, not with those trying to make the system work. This makes the default strategies used by school managers questionable, and in this respect it is right to look at the legacy of the linear, industrial process in play to ascertain why this is so. Most reforms are designed to fix special cause variation. The variation that most concerned Deming, however, is common cause variation and is the natural result of the system itself.

For most of the time, a system is fairly predictable and operates within expected parameters; it is under *control*, stable with only small fluctuations. It is designed to do a job, to work in the background. Such *common cause variation* for schools consists of the underpinning policies, practices, and procedures that inform the whole system and these define the work culture of the organization. But all of these are in turn governed by the limitations of the linear nature of the education process. For the most part, common cause variation results in an output distribution, which is at least stable over time. So, for schools, common cause variation is very much concerned with the linear nature of the school, the industrial inheritance.

The unpredictable output distortions of many schools can show an alarming degree of student underachievement, high drop-out rates, behavioral concerns, psychological problems, gang membership, health issues, low aspiration, poor attitude, low self-esteem, poor literacy skills, and so the list lengthens, off the charts. The unpredictable is now almost predictable in too many places. The high variation caused by social and economic challenges has revealed the frailty of linear (same-age) school systems as ones struggling to survive and being unable to adapt.

In almost all districts where high output variation exists, the remedies are a mess of politics, unionism, finance, ideology, and program reform to the point of managed overkill, but all to no avail. Education has become what some describe as *Swiss cheese*: learning full of holes; it is certainly a wicked mess. This means that any systems thinking ideas have to side-step current special cause and single-loop thinking and seek systemic alternatives. Schools have been unable to cope in a society increasingly divided and unequal in economics and life chances. The (d)elusion of the American Dream is wearing thin and this instability has started throw light on the inadequacies of the school system.

Schools simply faced a perfect storm. When social, environmental, and contextual complexity increase beyond normal working tolerances, system weaknesses in schools start to show. The systems learning process established in the previous century is stretched beyond its design parameters and is unable to adapt to the new conditions. It cannot self-organize. It lacks a double-loop learning feedback system and all of this leaves the teacher and the family isolated. Learning relationships, already variable, become close to unmanageable and learning starts to fail in critical areas centered directly on what appears to be the quality of the teacher (erroneous special cause).

Although most of the reasons for increased social complexity lie beyond the school gates, the school has to respond. However, when the school starts to fail as an organization, the mistake is to view the challenges (that *all* schools face) as being special cause variation and that these challenges can be fixed with pro-social program reforms, incentives, targets, and similar ideas. When the reforms ideas fail, the teachers are left to carry the can. This opens the door to another mess of unworkable ideas and proposed solutions. Throw in a recession or two and the perfect storm becomes a wicked mess.

Meanwhile, the school as an organization responds to the new and hyper-complex circumstances by lowering expectations, creating a special-needs industry, narrowing learning, and setting revised targets while proclaiming that no child should be left behind. And so, the waste accumulates, distortions remain high, flow gets blocked, and an impasse reached. The reformist and management approach is to see such output distortions as special cause variation, completely ignoring any entertainment of the view that it might be common cause variation that is the real problem. In effect, it is not the fault of teachers that it is the teacher's fault.

The whole approach to reform US style fails to make the distinction between special and common cause variation, and this not only limits success, but costs plenty. Special cause variation tends to be unpredictable and comprises strange and unexpected output distortions that focus on a complexity of standards and personnel issues. They bring out the scientific measurer in us, our preference for component part thinking. They invite data analysis and numbers, and these always suggest targets, management fixes, and revised accountabilities. Now look beyond the mess in the direction of common cause variation, a system unable to cope with rapid change, unable to be emergent.

Systems like schools are generally stable until environmental challenges create hyper-complex conditions that leave the school unable to adapt to changing ecological and contextual demands. Virtually all school output matters are actually common cause variation in origin—not special cause— but no one seems to have told reformers or the school!

The industrial model never needed much in the way of teamwork or communication; it remains organizationally unsophisticated. It interprets ideas about partnership and teamwork in orthodox ways long abandoned elsewhere. It responds to complexity by either creating more complexity, bureaucracy, and back-office systems or by dumbing down or both. It does not understand child psychology or customer care and is behind the ecological learning curve. It is full of magnificent people trying to hold together a system that is falling apart.

In schools, *common cause variation* appears to be operationally stable and most schools are able to achieve expected outcomes over time (the delusion or wicked problem). No action is deemed necessary. In jurisdictions where education is valued, in areas where students are compliant, in schools where there is a rigid disciplinary code, in schools fortunate to attract exceptional teachers, in schools where parents share school values, common cause variation goes unnoticed. The need for change is not seen in a world where all is special cause. Nevertheless, this organizational blind spot is still damaging to all, damaging to the commons. Making broken systems appear to work is clever but ultimately unhelpful, and this is the delusion created by the linear model.

Lynda Finn (2011) might describe all of this as a*cting inappropriately in the face of common cause variation.* The *cause* of the common cause variation is simply not recognized and so *special cause* solutions are preferred that fall in line with the orthodox solutions and *expertise* that have been built around our schools. Finn cites examples of applying special cause approaches to common cause problems and her examples are adapted here for schools. We might expect to see some of the following activities and we do!

- Observe the best teachers, schools, and systems; find out what they do that is different and copy them.
- Investigate why loads of things went wrong last week and look at what happened so it does not happen again.
- Send notices to school managers and teachers with higher-than-average failure rates asking them to improve their performance.
- Blame the situation on a particular individual; their replacement will fix the problem.
- Improve appraisal and introduce performance-related pay or simply increase pay all round.
- Find ways of giving parents simple online information to reduce their need to talk to school staff.
- Rank teachers on performance.

It is the stuff of modern school management but does not change the system. This *special cause* approach to an endemic *common cause* problem quickly leads to a "no-excuses" culture brilliantly described by Diane Ravitch (2012) in her review of the Finnish versus US education system. Rather than fix health, welfare, and poverty as outcomes of a broken system (common cause variation), the preference is to ignore these or see them as special cause variation in the way that teachers, school managers, and leaders are increasingly viewed. They can all be fixed by working harder, by offering more incentives, and by increasing accountability and training. Unfortunately, medicinal fixes for the wrong problems simply create junkies. As Ravitch (2012) says,

> The main mechanism of school reform today is to identify teachers who can raise their students' test scores every year. If the scores go up, reformers assume, then the students will enroll in college and poverty will eventually disappear. This will happen, the reformers believe, if there is a "great teacher" in every classroom. . . .

The trouble is that there is some truth here. There can be a great teacher in every classroom, but not in linear-dominated, factory-like school systems with such gross inattention to endemic common cause variation faults. By accepting the steady industrial state, adaptation fails alongside evolution. *Great teacher* infers great learning relationships and great learning relationships require a small design change capable of transforming the fundamentals, increasing interconnective communication flow, and redesigning the nature of common cause variation that is the main debilitating source of distorted human outputs.

The proposed answer to the common cause variation issue cannot be special cause in type; this merely constitutes another paradoxical dead end. To create better teachers requires system changes that enable them to be better, that enable learners to be better, and that can reach out to families who need the support of the school as much as the school needs them.

A broken system can be made to work by great teachers but most start to get chewed up by common cause variation long before they can attain greatness; they are then treated for the symptoms of special cause variation. The better long-term strategy to improve teacher quality involves understanding common cause variation management as a key strategic leadership skill. As Deming said, confusion between common causes and special causes leads to frustration for everyone, and leads to greater variability and to higher costs, contrary to what is needed.

BULLYING: SPECIAL CAUSE OR COMMON CAUSE VARIATION?

Having taken a glance at how common and special cause variation affects teachers, a little attention needs to be paid to the students and aspects of their behavior. Although antisocial behavior such as bullying is the chosen topic here, the ideas presented can transfer across the school.

This subtitle is generic. There are often unpredictable behaviors in and around schools that can affect learning. There is hardly a school, a district, or a jurisdiction that does not have in place a raft of anti-bullying policies, practices, procedures, counseling, and pro-social programs to deal with this problem. Schools work tirelessly to reduce and prevent such negative behaviors using control and support strategies of considerable imagination. And therein is the problem.

The strategies used to combat such behaviors are invariably special cause and rarely work as expected. Often the school separates them out as *pastoral* or counseling matters; repair strategies. If the many approaches used actually worked, bullying and antisocial behaviors would cease to be a concern, but that is clearly not the case. Given the huge weight of effort and cost put in and the damage caused, the changed behavior outputs remain hugely disappointing, a not unusual school output distortion: high reform and effort in, disappointing and unpredictable outcomes out.

The fundamental corrective strategies that schools operate to improve behavior may include anti-bullying strategies (policies, procedures, pro-social programs, citizenship courses, and operational practices based on ownership, respect, rights, etc.) to correct the anomaly, give the right support (perhaps counseling), and modify or prevent the errant behavior. All of these strategies assume that such output distortions can be treated as special cause variations and this severely limits success, that is, treat the students (special cause) not the system or even the family (common cause). How on earth could the school as an organization be the problem, especially because so much bullying and antisocial behavior begins life beyond the school's gates and seemingly beyond the school's reach?

The last thing a school and the many groups advising schools might consider is that many negative behaviors are exacerbated, or may even be caused by the system itself (i.e., they result in part from common cause variation issues that pertain to the underlying operational fundamentals and need to be treated as such). However, if they are treated as special cause it means that the system in operation is being ignored as a common cause party to the problem, which dilutes any remedial effect. In fact, the systems thinking proposal here is that most negative school behaviors cannot be successfully handled by normal practices (as special case) unless and until the underlying common cause issues are addressed.

In fact, the challenges that teachers face as teachers and students face as successful learners are almost entirely common cause in origin and unless that common cause is dealt with, operational flow can never be properly established and behaviors will occur that are counter to any understanding of positive psychology. Because everyone is differentially affected by whatever their work circumstances are, a system that is itself unhealthy passes on any damaging effects to those working in it. Psychology, good relationships, communication, shared purpose, support, and information are all vital components that help us do well and all are double-loop, common cause matters. Their absence or assumed presence is damaging.

Deming (1994) suggested in his theory of profound knowledge, four interconnected understandings; appreciation of a system, knowledge of variation, theory of knowledge, and psychology. When critically applied to the school's linear systems structure, it quickly becomes clear that such a system cannot effectively meet psychological needs, that common cause variation has been misunderstood or ignored, and that the theory of knowledge that schools claim is not as coherent as it seems. How and why this is the case is discussed in subsequent chapters, but an example is offered here.

When students join a school and a school organizes special cause approaches (team activities, launch days, and getting-to-know-you games to win loyalty and confidence) they are also creating the potential for group formations that can be as much negative as positive. Schools do not see the dangers of such one-off settling-in strategies. We assume that this is what will make children happy and confident learners. Schools believe they are developing positive behaviors and good social relationships; if only it were all so simple. So many of our organizational assumptions regarding the needs of children are simply wrong. Schools, in trying to do the right thing, too often organize the jungle where Ralph, Piggy, and the other kids play and must try and seek like-minded allies to survive.

Through a small system redesign to correct aspects of common cause variation, much of the negative and bullying behavior dissipates, revealing the real and residual special cause variation that warrants the school's attention. Again, it is a question of abandoning the linear model to build immediate and long-term measures relating to learning and support process relationships (VT). The psychology and method as to the *how* and the *why* this is so, is set out in the next chapter and chapters to come.

Suffice it to say, those secondary schools that introduce a non-programmed, vertical dimension (mixed age or VT) almost without exception report a significant reduction in bullying and, by implication, gang membership. It requires no pro-social taught program, but it does require a systems thinking approach to the set-up and the design process; a basic systems understanding of how the components of Deming's theory of profound knowledge work together to create a system. Part of that process is to fulfill a child's need to belong to a group that cares for that child and part of that process is forming a child–tutor relationship before and above any teaching activity.

THE INDUSTRIAL OR FACTORY MODEL

What defines the factory view of schools is not domineering teachers and passive children set in serried rows being made to learn irrelevant information to pass standardized tests, but a fragile and limited, linear single-loop sorting culture that prevents the essential socio-psychological interconnections between school, child, and family from forming into a fully operational teaching and learning system. It is a place of single, closed-loop practice of repeated special cause strategies designed for an earlier time and place. A highly effective learning operation requires an open double-loop learning process that is able to monitor, regulate, and work with common cause variation.

E. D. Hirsch (1999) set out a masterful analysis of school reform as confused *romantic progressivism*. In many ways he identified the end game of the failure of reform to identify and deal with common cause variation and systemic change issues.

It is not so much that schools have resisted reform; far from it. They have actually been buffeted by the unceasing change inputs despite no fundamental redesign being demanded of the faulty and inflexible common cause variation inherent in the linear model. What the reform movement has done is caused an already fragile single-loop learning school to be tossed around in a sea of half-thought-out ideas and assumptions that have deprived schools of their sense of purpose and created an inability to distinguish good practice from bad. Rather than be helpful to teachers, Hirsch suggests that *progressive-romantic* ideas have made our schools look incompetent and flirtatious with failure.

There is a good case for suggesting that the preoccupation with special cause variation may well have spawned what Hirsch calls "the Thoughtworld's intellectual dominance." His chapter titled "Critical Guide to Educational Terms and Phrases" should be pinned to every staffroom wall, not only as a think piece and part of the school's deprogramming and unlearning process, but as a learning process too. From a systems thinking point of view, instead of being connected to parents, to students, and to more of themselves, schools appear to have formed a quasi-alliance with a *Thoughtworld* of so-called progressive and romantic reform ideas and some unhelpful interpretations of research.

As Hirsch says,

> Prospective teachers and members of the general public are bemused, bullied, and sometimes infected by seductive rhetorical flourishes like "child centered schooling" or bullying ones like "drill and kill." These terms and phrases pretend no more soundness, humaneness, substance and scientific authority than they in fact possess. Promulgating this system of rhetoric has been an ongoing function of American schools of education, whose uniformity of lan-

guage and doctrine ensures that every captive of the teacher-certification process and every professor trained to continue the tradition is imbued with educationally correct phrases. Consensus-through-rhetoric has been one of the
main instruments of the Thoughtworld's dominance.

For this book, the kind of romanticism Hirsch suggests is more distortion—
an extension of the common cause and special cause variation problem—but
it is one that continues to buffet schools and confuse purpose. We must be
conscious that VT has not been a consideration in these heady arguments in
the United States and may come across as another reform oddity; otherwise,
the focus rages inadvertently, inappropriately, and continuously on frustra-
tions within the classroom and with teacher capability and fault, and this
denies any sensible resolution by any common cause definition.

Systems thinking is able to do much to get schools working better as
organizations prior to full systemic change. It is a question of creating a
school that respects the commons of which schools are an integral part. Peter
Senge (2006) offers us clues from *The Fifth Dimension*: "Manage the commons either through educating everyone or creating forms of self-regulation
and peer pressure or through an official regulating mechanism, ideally designed by the participants." We can do this if the school is systems thinking.

Chapter Eight

Child Development, Customer Care, and Adaptive Systems Thinking

> A leader of transformation, and managers involved, need to learn the psychology of individuals, the psychology of a group, the psychology of society, and the psychology of change.
>
> —W. Edwards Deming, 1986

Systems thinking teaches us that everything is connected. A school must be directly connected to and compatible with other systems. It cannot act in isolation; it must have a purpose and a process that all understand and one to which all can contribute. It is both its own commons and part of the bigger commons, what we inherit and what we create, all at the same time. Otherwise, it becomes ecologically disconnected and purpose is lost, which seems to be where we find ourselves.

Psychology here is confined to two main areas. The first involves in-group loyalty, the idea that we are all members of groups that guide our beliefs and powerfully influence our behaviors; this is especially so for children. In-group loyalty refers to the many influential *belonging* groups such as family, friends, ethnicity, religion, culture, peers, and even gangs, all of which exert a powerful influence on what Robert McCrae (2007) termed "openness to experience." The second involves a simple summation of what we understand by child development and the role of the school and the family within the child development process.

In this respect, our teachers and everyone else know that children arrive at school as long-standing members of influential groups, many of which do not universally sing the praises of school values. At school, such groups can expand, reform, and grow in impact, often with a detrimental effect on learning and especially so if in-group loyalty is negative with regard to schooling

(Edwards and D'arcy 2004). This can create an in-group loyalty clash requiring intervention, so one area of inquiry is a test on the effectiveness of the school to do this, and to enable positive in-group loyalty to replace negative.

The other component of psychology refers to the significant role that adults play in child development and especially the main caregivers at home and at school. Murray Bowen (1978) suggests that the basic emotional unit consists of two people, but because this is an unstable structure, it requires a third party to create balance. His family systems theory seems to be similar in form to aspects of systems thinking insofar as it is not possible to understand an individual's behavior in isolation from other family members, the rest of the system.

The family requires triangular feedback loops that constantly form and reform as needed to make progress and maintain equilibrium. The business of emotional and learning support triangles crops up many times in this book in the form of learning relationships and support feedback loops. The formation of these triangular, double-looped group mechanisms is one of the keys to the basic design strategy pertaining to the thinking systems school and is set out in detail later.

Rather than give a lengthy overview on child psychology (well beyond my expertise), it is important to hone in on the essentials, and here, the work of Bronfenbrenner is used as our guide: systems thinking looks for interconnectedness and in particular the positive supportive relationships between school, home, and the child, which Bronfenbrenner's work (1977, 1979) encapsulates.

Customer care is dealt with in greater detail later as one of the most important knowledge and management areas needed to create and design the systems thinking school. It refers to the idea that everyone in and connected to the school is a customer of everyone else. All have demands and all offer essential services; all are trying to operate within the complex information and communication exchange that comprises the school.

THE CHILD AND THE SCHOOL

In operational terms, psychology should inform and help enable the design of a systems thinking school. It should do this by telling us what is needed and what is essential for the characters in this play to perform and learn at their best.

It is Ludwig Von Bertalanffy who invited us to think again about thinking. He defined a general system as any theoretical system that might be of interest to multiple disciplines. He includes growth and evolution as examples, all of which feature interrelated properties able to transcend the orthodox boundaries of disciplines. For Bertalanffy (1968) people are *active per-*

sonality systems crossing boundaries of biology, psychology, sociology, etc. In this way it is helpful to think of childhood as a dynamic and emergent system in its own right.

Looking at child growth as a kind of system, it is clearly one that is formed and shaped by interaction with other people and other systems like family, school, friends, and wider society. It receives and is honed by influential feedback loops and masses of information that require processing. The family *system* and the school *system* eventually meet up to share learning responsibilities for the child system and ongoing child development. Both family and school are influential hierarchical systems and both shoulder responsibilities for successful schooling. Donella Meadows (2009) put it this way:

> To be a highly functional system, hierarchy must balance the welfare, freedoms, and responsibilities of the subsystems and total system—there must be enough central control to achieve coordination towards the large system goal, and enough autonomy to keep the subsystems flourishing, functioning and self-organizing.

Such a statement tells us much about the psychological balance a school system must aspire to.

During the school stage, a child cannot simply flit between home and school as though these were two separate systems. There has to be interconnectivity and a commonality of purpose between home and school. The purpose of home and school from a systems perspective is to enable the child to be *self-organizing*, able to learn, diversify, and adapt. When school, child, and home interconnect, they form an optimal learning system itself connected to a larger social system and so on. In other words, systems should be adaptive, able to self-organize and evolve.

An *active personality system* is capable of accepting challenges, solving problems, and engaging in artistic expression (a bit like most kids really). As open systems, all kinds of social and ecological interactions come into play. Kids learn all sorts of things; they are open to experience (good and bad), are constantly engaging with information and communication skills and responding to their desire to be in groups (in-group loyalty). They can also affect their environment just as their environment affects them.

Beyond the school gates and brought into the school are other potent social and ecological pressures that influence a child's openness to experience and to learning: media, social networks, neighborhoods, friends, gangs, family, etc. On entry to school at any level, the child is already a card-carrying member of powerful loyalty groups of which family and friends (peers) are particularly influential.

The child is about to enter a school situation in which new loyalty groups form and old ones can grow, two systems meeting: one an active personality system and the other a hierarchical system packed with procedures and practices all loaded with a compliancy of rules and policies and dominated by the clock. Each has to get the best out of the other and just as children present themselves in a variety of ways, so do schools. Learning is not just a function of the school or classroom nor is it the only place where knowledge is accrued and synthesized. The school is part of a wider learning process, but it comprises the one where most life chances weigh in the balance.

THE CHILD AND THE FAMILY SYSTEM

The active personality system of the child learns and continuously adapts, and the greatest influence on that process is the family, or should be. Childhood can be a vulnerable time open to debilitating and long-term damage; there is much that can go wrong and the family invariably provides the support framework needed to get the child through.

To understand Bertalanffy's active personality system, we have to appreciate what is happening in the family in terms of behaviors and relationships. Ask any school counselor or head of pastoral care why the child behaves in the way he or she does, and they may well cast a wary eye toward the family! Schools know that the family is a powerful system of interconnected and interdependent members, each with roles to play and each adhering to unwritten relationship rules (Bowen 1978). Avid followers (like me) of TV programs such as *Cheers, The Sopranos*, and *House* are intrigued by family and relationships. For my partner, *Desperate Housewives* and *Sex and the City* are her preferred tipple. We are social animals, curious and gossipy even though it is estimated that 90 percent of our communication is non-verbal in form.

Families have a defining characteristic. Any change in a single family member affects the rest of the family system. The intent of the resilient family is to keep things stable, constantly trying to return to normal following any deviation, a system construct of homeostasis. In some ways, families too have to cope with demand and manage variation, but no matter what happens, the slightest change and everyone is affected—a causal systems circularity. *It's not you, it's me. It's never just you! Nobody is an island.*

Systems thinking models and feedback loops help us stand back and see such connections, a point made by Martha Cox and Blair Paley (1997): "models are helpful for considering multiple influences on (child) development and adaptation and have implications for the design of effective interventions." This is important for the redesign process later.

All of these psychological factors form the basis for any school design and have to be built into the school's learning system not added on. The first consideration of the school is how to connect an adult from the school with the child in a real and substantive way. Bronfenbrenner explains why this is so.

Bronfenbrenner's theories are not only important for schools but also help to explain the many organizational challenges that schools face; but then Bronfenbrenner is a systems thinker.

BIO-ECOLOGICAL SYSTEMS THEORY

Bronfenbrenner takes us to the basic nature and nurture debate and applies systems thinking to this question: "As the child grows, how does the world that surrounds that child help or hinder the child's continued development?" Bronfenbrenner (1977, 1979) begins by identifying ecological structures conceptually similar to the work of Abraham Maslow (1943). The *bi-directional* descriptor given here refers to the idea that change always has a two-way effect.

Like Maslow, Bronfenbrenner draws a picture of the child's world, a system of *nested* influences and interrelationships that affect the child's development.

1. The microsystem is the layer closest to the child and is the most influential. Here are the primary two-way relationships and interactions with family, school, neighborhood, child care, etc. This is where the two-way (bi-directional) influence is strongest, although these can occur throughout and between ecological layers.
2. The mesosystem provides connections between the structures that make up the microsystem, such as the connection between home and school.
3. The exosystem is the wider social system. This is often the parental world of employment. Although seemingly detached from this environment, there is nevertheless a powerful force that can interact with the child's microsystem, such as parental income and work hours.
4. The macrosystem is the outer layer of customs, laws, and values. These too can permeate other layers and influence the child's micro level.
5. The chronosystem is like a calendar. Puberty and cognition (internal) and significant events (e.g., a parent's death) impact here.

Bronfenbrenner uses this bio-ecological model to explain why so many families are under stress. Family life has been allowed to struggle on despite the

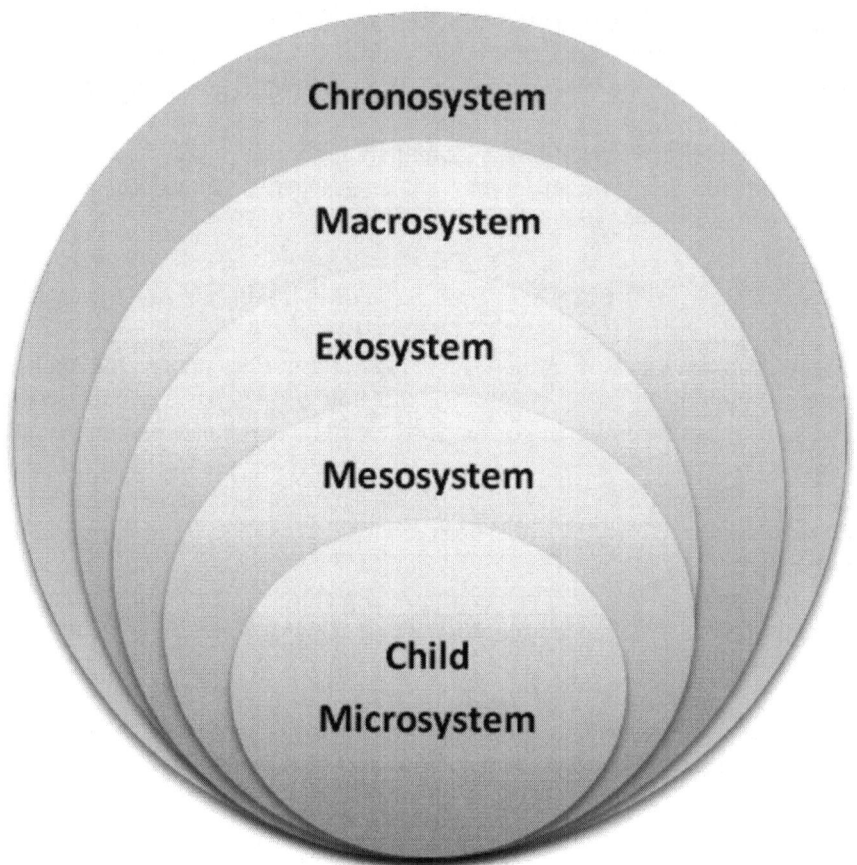

Figure 8.1.

damage caused by the invasive changes that technology brings. Although the economy has largely shifted from an industrial model to a knowledge economy, the workplace (including the child's school workplace) continues to rely on factory work ethics and practices. In fact, far from setting people free from time and place issues, the work ethic demands more *face time* than ever.

As more women enter the workforce they too are affected, and all of this, according to Bronfenbrenner, has had a detrimental effect on family life and on the positive growth chances of children. The home is too often an abandoned place, a brief rest point in the busy lives of people under pressure, instead of being a place where people meet up to make sense of the world and establish the homeostasis they need to grow. In many respects the resilience of the family has been weakened. Add recession to this and it is clear that banks are not the only institutions to be stress tested.

What is important here is the degree of match between the child's developmental needs and the school's response in ensuring that the mesosystem can function and is not ignored or downplayed. In effect, the school is an important part of the child's developmental process and especially so when family life is under strain. For Bronfenbrenner there has been considerable damage to families and family life and this means that schools have to be aware of this when designing all aspects of schooling to ensure all children have access to individual support and guidance not just the few. He is talking about interconnectivity; systems working in harmony.

In the United States, 20 percent of children live in poverty, school dropout rates are disproportionally high, and access to health care for many is abysmally low. School outcomes are not good! According to Bronfenbrenner, there has been mass disruption to the child's microsystem, and technological change has caused families to become unpredictable and less stable as bi-directional impact cuts in (Figure 8.1). Bronfenbrenner sees this ecological disruption as the most destructive force in a child's development.

When a child's microsystem implodes, is damaged, or suddenly changes, the child does not have the capabilities and wherewithal to explore other parts of the wider environment, and openness to learning is restricted or damaged. For Bronfenbrenner, the *Headstart* program he provided formed an essential part of the critical intervention needed. In 1990, Bronfenbrenner set out five propositions to describe the processes that foster the development of human competence and character. At the core of these propositions is a child's emotional, physical, intellectual, and social need for ongoing mutual interaction with a caring adult, and preferably with many adults.

These propositions need to be read with care and with school design in mind. If Bronfenbrenner is right, then these propositions need to be recognized and incorporated into the design of any systems thinking school. In all respects these propositions must be in sync with the school's supply-side capability and communication function; otherwise, the two systems (school and child) will not connect properly and each can damage the other. In such a clash, the growth of both systems is affected. The child loses life chances and the school loses the chance to benefit from revealing the talents that the child had to offer; and so does society.

Later, the view will be presented that school compensatory systems to handle system fall-out damage, such as pastoral care and counseling, are insufficient in themselves because these assume such matters are special cause variation. Counseling a child may be necessary and useful, but this special cause approach invariably masks a deeper systemic problem; it is insufficient for the job that needs to be done. Bullying is not an individual or group problem alone; it is another single-loop system distortion more easily resolvable by designing interconnectivity in, preventative rather than after the fact. Meanwhile, note should be made of the many references to adult relationships as essential for successful child growth, an area we and our children have been erroneously trained to treat with great suspicion, increasing risk and harm rather than reducing it.

In many ways Bronfenbrenner has set out the essential social, emotional, and psychological foundations that need to be inherent in a systems thinking school, characteristics that should shine through in the way a school organizes itself and its key learning relationships. These propositions guide the role that caring and responsible adults play in the lives of young people and the constant need for communication and affirmation to ensure that the bio-

---

The Five Critical Processes for Positive Development
"I am sometimes asked up to what age do these principles apply. The answer is debatable, but I would say anytime up to the age of, say, 99." *Uri* Bronfenbrenner
Proposition 1. In order to develop intellectually, emotionally, socially, and morally ...a child requires participation in progressively more complex reciprocal activity, on a regular basis over an extended period in the child's life, with one or more persons with whom the child develops a strong, mutual, emotional attachment and who is committed to the child's well-being and development, preferably for life.
Proposition 2. The establishment of patterns of progressive interpersonal interaction under conditions of strong mutual attachment enhances the young child's responsiveness to other features of the immediate physical, social, and - in due course - symbolic environment that invite exploration, manipulation, elaboration and imagination. Such activities, in turn, also accelerate the child's psychological growth.
Proposition 3. The establishment and maintenance of patterns of progressively more complex interaction and emotional attachment between caregiver and child depend in substantial degree on the availability and involvement of another adult, a *third party* who assists, encourages, spells off, gives status to, and expresses admiration and affection for the person caring for and engaging in joint activity with the child.
Proposition 4. The effective functioning of child-rearing processes in the family and other child settings requires establishing ongoing patterns of exchange of information, two-way communication, mutual accommodation, and mutual trust between the principal settings in which children and their parents live their lives. These settings are the home, child-care programs, the school, and the parents' place of work.
Proposition 5. The effective functioning of child-rearing processes in the family and other child settings requires public policies and practices that provide place, time, stability, status, recognition, belief systems, customs, and actions in support of child-rearing activities not only on the part of parents, caregivers, teachers, and other professional personnel, but also relatives, friends, neighbours, co-workers, communities, and the major economic, social, and political institutions of the entire society.
"Discovering What Families Do" by Urie Bronfenbrenner in Rebuilding the Nest: A New Commitment to the American Family, published by Family Service America, 1990.

Figure 8.2.

ecological system functions—systems supporting systems and interconnecting. In social psychology, this can be interpreted in part as the need to build positive in-group loyalty with and around young people.

Such reciprocity stabilizes the dynamics of the child's bio-ecological environment, their world, enabling self-organization. When people talk about the idea that it takes a village to raise a child, they are talking about many adults advising, mentoring, teaching, and affirming, while providing the consistency and range of support that best inspire confidence and motivation.

ENTER THE CHILD'S TUTOR AT PROPOSITION 3

Readers are invited to look closely at Bronfenbrenner's propositions and especially at Proposition 3 (Figure 8.2). This describes parent partnership and the essential in-group loyalty of the parent, school, and child triangle. We now need to replace the word *school* in the previous sentence with the word *tutor* to underpin the adult role in child development. Here then is the stable building block that allows the child to *boldly go*.

It is the same triangle that arose out of the systems check. On day one, the induction day, on the first day of secondary school, when a school accepts a student and a student accepts a school, this adult-child (home-school) relationship requires immediate attention if it is to form and cannot be abandoned in the name of team-building exercises and getting-to-know-you games that can so easily allow negative in-group loyalties to run amok without intervention. Neither can it wait for teachers to perform their magic. The industrial model can no longer be allowed take destructive human risks using the support mechanisms it erroneously promotes.

At the heart of the systems thinking school is a familiar person (the student's tutor) who sees the child every day, who knows that child well, who can monitor performance, who can support learning, who can engage the mentoring help of older children, who can intervene quickly, and who shares with parents the fulfillment of Bronfenbrenner's propositions. This front-office relationship between child and tutor and parents needs to form and be facilitated immediately on entry to the school and certainly well before the child goes to the classroom.

This VT or mixed-age group tutoring is small group, intimate time when a new student meets their tutors (usually two) and selected students. It is one of the first things that should happen on entry and takes about twenty minutes. Only then can the school consider team games and getting-to-know-you exercises, although these will not really be needed. Only then is the child able to explore other avenues with confidence. He or she can then play the social games and go to the classroom—and only then!

In Proposition 4, Bronfenbrenner sets out the communications design requirement for the systems thinking school, a proposition that makes intuitive and subjective systems thinking sense. What schools need to understand is why this is and then how best to do it! This too is set out in later chapters. Failure to do so comes at a high price. In a powerful article in the *RSA Journal*, Susie Orbach (2012) described the critical need for early intervention for the many families in desperate need of support where

> mental health problems, learning difficulties and violence in early family life all set patterns that are hard to treat, dissolve and dislodge unless engaged with early on. . . . Our city centres are full of youngsters whose hurt feelings were never addressed in their early years. Their distress sits like a rocket ready to explode.

The few are becoming the many. It is all too easy for the child's aspiration gene to diminish; to send them to the classroom first and ask questions later; to rely on compliance with the school's industrial and linear system. Children seek affirmation in their relationships with significant adults (parents and teachers), and if that is absent or takes an age to develop, they may seek it in the inappropriate and darker places of cyberspace, the 'hood and in gangs. Bronfenbrenner is not shy about the dire implications for schools and teachers.

If it is the broken relationship between the workplace and home that is the distorted outcome caused by conflict between technological change and industrial thinking, then it is the relationship between the school and the home that must play the essential role in the healing. To grow and develop, the child requires long-term stability and caring, a complexity of interaction from an immediate primary adult—preferably more than one.

If the technological world is the root cause of so many problems impacting on a child's microsystem, then the child's school and the child's family must form a real partnership of trust if the growing child is to learn and thrive. They must be interconnected and schools have to understand that this systems function is critical to growth and to learning. But this applies to all children not the dysfunctional, broken few. Schools absolutely must ensure their industrial ways no longer create a technological problem, and that means changing the way our schools are managed.

MORE BLOCKAGES TO FLOW

The tragedy is that the factory school cannot properly perform this vital function given the school's organizational restrictions in one of many crucial areas. The linear horizontal year system or grade system that forms the resistant unbending basis of the industrial school model *cannot* flex enough to meet students' psychological needs. This endangers the child by abandoning them to the world of the classroom where learning and teaching are separated from the totality of the school and home. Such systems are destined to fail again and again when faced with complexity and new demands and cannot be fixed by pro-social programs and add-ons. Indeed these fixes, all of them, increase the potential for damage and have been made worse by viewing adults as potential dangers, *stranger dangers*, and suspect interlopers in the child's world.

The systems thinking school has to run its learning process differently, securely, and more flexibly so that care and quality are *built in* and never added on and in such a way that no child ever feels unsupported. Such a systems approach must be proactive, not reactive.

There is a deep common cause variation problem in our linear school model that creates distortions in learning relationships, a reliance on invalid assumptions about child growth and an ecological separation from values. We have been unable to access the knowledge required to understand the wicked problem; without this, trust has broken down and the confidence to embark on systemic change has stalled. Our industrial teaching model is an abusive entity delivering exam results as a poor substitute for learning.

LIFE CYCLE DECLINE

We have reached the point that Madhukar Shukla (1994) identified so well, when one paradigm should be coming to an end and giving way to another. Shukla was looking at corporations but schools and districts can learn much from his analysis. The vital signs do not bode well for linear schools. The comments in parentheses are my interpretation.

Reasons for Corporate (School) Failure	Underlying Learning Disabilities
1.Life-Cycle Decline	Inadequate ecological scanning and internal competency building (Schools out of synch with environment)
2.Trapped by Past Success	Complacency and arrogance leading to rigidity and lack of openness to knowledge (Insular leadership: increase in command and control leadership methods)
3. Inappropriate Strategic Biases and Mental Models	Lack of self-critiquing and self-reflection causing misalignment with the environment (Schools unable to analyze themselves [unlearn] while closed systems prevent self-emergence and adaptation. No systems thinking skills: customers alienated)
4. Rigidity in Response to a Crisis	Defensive and self-destructive routines and practices hampering adaptive responses (System unable to respond to common cause variation: reform and repair fails: mass build up of waste preventing flow)

Figure 8.3.

The reasons for corporate failure set out by Shukla (Figure 8.3) help describe where schools are. Shukla was not researching schools, but the similarities with other organizations are striking. They need little explanation and are discussed in greater detail in my book, *Vertical Tutoring: Notes on School Management, Learning Relationships and School Improvement.* All of these are a mixture of common cause variation and the distortions caused by an inability to adapt. The underlying learning disability is actually single-loop thinking trying to cope in a complex double-loop world. The single loops grew out of a linear model in a simpler time that never needed to ask the deeper questions. Our schools are precisely at this point, but the delusions emanating from the system and the orthodoxy that pertains simply do not see such a reality and do not yet perceive viable systemic alternatives.

In this twilight time between paradigm shifts, we have to show schools that they can improve outputs (academically, socially, and psychologically) by being learning-driven and values-driven, even though we are unlikely to wean the system entirely of its testing and target-setting mentality. This means reconnecting people within a better designed learning process relevant to this century rather than the last. We can make a start by putting the key pieces of the systems thinking jigsaw puzzle together.

Chapter Nine

The Systems Thinking School: First Principles and Interconnectivity

[T]here is little opportunity for sustained conversation between student and teacher. . . . One must infer that careful probing of students' thinking is not a high priority.

—Ted Sizer, 1984

Having considered family, school, and child as separate systems, all three must somehow garner their responsibilities and form a learning system. It is no longer possible to separate responsibilities for child development as the industrial model seeks to do; the danger of poor or reduced outcomes is too great. In all respects, each is linked to the other and together must be viewed as a single interconnected learning system.

Fiona Carnie (2004) concluded her book on child-friendly schools with a number of thoughts. Let's hear it again for the parent customer, the parent's story.

Opportunities for parents to contribute in a meaningful way to what goes on within their children's school are inadequate. . . . And yet parents know as well, if not better than anyone, how their children feel about school and, consequently, how things might be improved.

It is for schools to take the initiative on how such a partnership arrangement forms; any imposition from the outside will seem like yet another reform, an add-on in a world of add-ons. Such a revised design, however, cannot involve a rearrangement of all that passes as current practice; it has to be systemic and be guided by clear values and management principles, many of which have already been revealed in previous chapters.

The challenge is to create a system that inspires learning, meets the demands of parents, recognizes the psychological and learning needs of students, and enables better teaching. It simply cannot remain the case that around a quarter to a third of US public high school students drop out and that an even higher percentage of blacks, Hispanics, and American Indians fail to graduate (Swanson 2004). The High School Dropouts in America (2012) survey, albeit a sample, listed various reasons for such a dropout rate. These included lack of parental support or encouragement (23 percent), entering parenthood (21 percent), and missing too much school (17 percent) followed closely by failing in class, uninteresting classes, mental illness, and bullying.

There is much to be learned from the reasons that students give for dropping out of school. The study by Civic Enterprises for the Bill and Melinda Gates Foundation, *The Silent Epidemic: Perspectives of High School Dropouts* (Bridgeland et al. 2006), lists the usual suspects of boredom, missed days, negative peer influence, too much freedom and not enough rules, and so on. It seems that a confusion of negative forces is at work that eventually wrestles them from school and keeps the United States near the foot of the OECD table for dropouts and failure to graduate. Like so many reports, it calls in vain for policy makers to act.

However, it is what these same young people suggest could help that is so important. It seems that most of what students need is (with a little systems thinking support) well within the remit of schools. Although students are willing to admit that they made bad decisions and feel that they can only blame themselves, they suggest five actions that may have turned things around; schools should take note:

- Make school more engaging through real-world, experiential learning. Students want to see the connection between school and work.
- Improve instruction and support for struggling learners. These include better teachers, smaller classes, more individualized instruction, more tutoring, and extra time with teachers.
- Improve school climate. A majority of students believed that schools need greater supervision and classroom discipline. More than half said schools should do more to protect students from violence.
- Ensure that students have a relationship with at least one adult in the school. Only 56 percent of students said that they could go to a member of the staff for help with school problems; only 41 percent said that they could talk to an adult in their school about personal problems.
- Improve communication between parents and schools. Fewer than half of students said that their schools had contacted them or their parents when they were absent or had dropped out.

The first recommendation asks that the ecological link be reformed, something system thinkers also desire. There has to be greater relevance and purpose. There has to be a minimum core of learning early on that students must establish. Children cannot progress to secondary level without basics in place. Any upstream failure in learning becomes an expensive and major challenge downstream (Pasmore 1988). Changes of school phases and the possibility of abrogated responsibility by individual schools for learning are not desirable. Middle school and high school separation is not appropriate and appears to be endorsed for dubious reasons of resourcing rather than all-through learning and stronger learning relationships. These are the matters for policy makers.

It is the last four bullet points that matter here. Each and every one is within the remit of schools and virtually at zero cost. It is the managerial unlearning required to make the subtle changes that is important and challenging.

SCHOOL DESIGN: A BLUEPRINT

Resolution of this wicked dropout problem may not be easy, but in this case and every case, proactive and rapid intervention and prevention is better than downstream reaction. The former is economic and aids flow, and the latter is hugely expensive and accumulates waste. The latter then undermines the former, so getting any system change right first time always wins.

It is understanding the simplicity that is complex! Any approach with managers has to change. The ideas set out require unlearning and re-learning because they are all systems thinking in essence, managing the whole system not faulting and trying to manage the individuals who comprise the system. That can only happen once the system is running properly. Basically, the linear model needs attention; the people in it need healing; the children are asking for better support and encouragement from adults, the parents need help and want to be involved, and the teachers and school staff need to understand that learning is a full systemic operational matter, a shared activity of shared responsibilities.

To achieve these things the school needs to be *vertically re-cultured*.

In the previous chapter the tutor entered the frame in part to recognize such concerns and to rebuild the missing connectivity needed by the system participants. This means that our systems thinking school will need to adopt a key management principle. In effect, we have taken a good, long look at the linear system, conducted a systems check, observed the actors in our play, and gathered a picture of what appears to be happening from a systems thinking perspective.

It should now be possible to map out a first blue print for a school design, sketching in the key changes, management principles, and inherent values. The purpose at this stage is get the school as a system operating in a coherent way and one that best supports learning and teaching. The way a school works operationally will impact directly how students, and especially the most vulnerable, engage with learning. Herewith is the basic blueprint; details follow:

1. Almost everybody working in a school, in whatever capacity and regardless of status, should be a tutor attached to a tutor or home group. This includes office staff and the principal. The tutors stay with their tutees throughout their time at school. Nobody should ever join the school in any capacity without realizing that they will be expected to be a tutor.
2. The home group should meet daily, before break, for about twenty minutes. Each home group has two tutors attached. Tutors or mentors do not teach or deliver pro-social programs.
3. The tutor group is reduced in size to twenty or less and contains children of all ages. There should be no more than four students from a single grade or year.
4. A nested system will be introduced. Older students will often work with younger ones. Tutor groups are attached to houses or colleges, and these form the larger school: schools within schools.

The first domino involves dismantling the linear grade system as the organizational system form. From this point, everything changes, provided there is sufficient systems knowledge. The effect of these first principles changes every single facet of school management and learning support when implemented and understood: the start of a complete cultural and systems makeover. These changes ensure that the school is set up in a way that is psychologically sound and supportive and better suited to meet customer care needs; it is customer care that now needs attention.

THE TUTOR AS A LEARNING CONDUIT

The changes enumerated highlight a proactive management shift. The tutors, not the teachers, are now the key learning conduit between home and school, and it the tutors' close relationships with the students that are of paramount importance. The challenge for management is to redesign a learning process that establishes the tutors and the parents as key participants. The tutors should, in effect, become the school's front offices, each handling the essential information, intervention, and learning support that students need. The task of managers is to ensure that students get what they need: tutors who know them well as young people, tutors who support their learning needs, tutors who care passionately about their success, tutors able to listen and mentor, and tutors who liaise with home.

One of the many subtle changes that managers must make is to enable the tutor-based front-office system to draw down resources from a streamlined back office, thus enabling rapid intervention and better learning support. To achieve this operational front-office learning support system, teachers must supply information that informs grades *and* learning, not grades alone. In some respects, a tutor and a parent can only be as effective as the quality of information they receive. This means changes to the assessment and reporting process as all aspects of interaction become more bespoke and personalized. This might mean *strategies for improvement* rather than simply *targets for achievement*; information that enables a team approach. This makes the relationship between tutor and student all important.

It is appreciated that these seemingly simple changes require far more thought and training than it seems. To simply make such changes without a clear idea of the rationale behind them is to invite disaster. These changes affect common cause variation in a substantive way, by designing in a front-office and double-loop feedback and communication process. When this is done, what remains is special cause variation; this change acts to remove delusion from the system along with any distortions. The mischievous ghost in the machine is, in effect, busted!

The homeroom tutor no longer has a homogeneous group of same-age pupils composed of powerful subgroups and unpredictable in-group loyalties (again a common cause problem, system not personnel). This is replaced by a smaller home group (tutor group) comprised of mixed-age students where support for learning and positive, pro-social in-group loyalty can be better achieved. How this is done is explained throughout the following chapters, but it always requires management knowledge, training, and sound leadership skills.

Where previously, key learning relationships took an age to build if they built at all, they can now be virtually guaranteed from day one, built in not added on. This is important because time is something kids and parents do not have. In fact, the tutor is faced with a completely different set of social and learning circumstances and no taught program to lean on. How exciting is that? Of course there is a preparation and training issue, but nothing that demands anything more of home group tutors than to be the people that the kids need them to be.

In this win-win situation, parents, students, teachers, and tutors all benefit. In later chapters, we can start to put these systems thinking principles and values together. Meanwhile, the parents now have a first point of contact for the first time and so does everyone else. It is simply a question of building the new management structures around the redesigned learning process so that all parties remain connected, informed, involved, and empowered.

For schools, this means looking again at purpose, values, and principles and being guided by psychology and customer care. Much of the domino effect requires a system that draws together people made separate by the industrial, linear model and its residual management ideas. It is the idea of interconnection that is so important and which is so powerfully reflected in the needs identified in the dropout survey. The basic model is set out here:

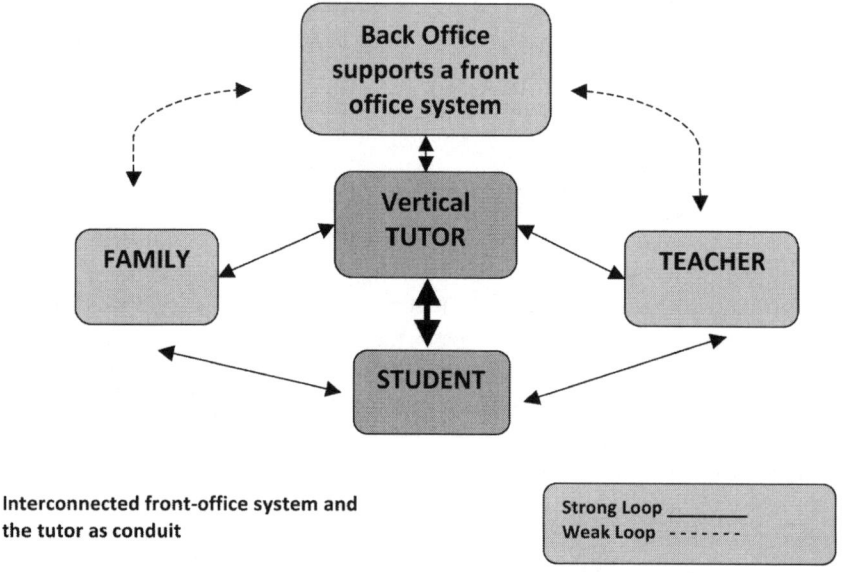

Interconnected front-office system and the tutor as conduit

Strong Loop _____
Weak Loop - - - - - -

NB. In this non-linear model or double-loop system, the linear process has been redesigned. Every child now has a personal tutor (two in fact) whom they see on a daily basis. The parent has a first port of call direct with the school through this new front-office, tutor-based system. The teacher (all of whom are also tutors) has access to information that enables her to build learning relationships far more quickly given that the tutor has already done this prior to the child going to the classroom. Within tutor time, older and younger students are encouraged to work together as needed, recreating familial partnership relationships within the school. The home group has become a home group! All players are now working as and for, Team Child.

Figure 9.1.

It should be noted that books on systems thinking are often obsessed with loops to clarify how systems function. Hopefully, this one is relatively simple!

There are few written models around to guide schools on what such a management system might look like, but an exception exists at the Mount Edgecombe High School in Alaska (Figure 9.2).

Our actions are based on the following beliefs
1. Human relations are the foundation for all quality improvement
2. All components of our organisation can be improved
3. Removing the causes of problems in the system inevitably leads to improvement
4. The person doing the job is the most knowledgeable about the job
5. People want to be involved and do their jobs well
6. Every person wants to feel like a valued contributor
7. More can be accomplished by working together to improve the system than by working individually around the system
8. A structured process using statistical graphic problem-solving techniques lets you know where you are, where the variations lie, the relative importance of the problems to be solved, and whether the changes made have had a desired impact
9. Adversarial relationships are counterproductive and outmoded
10. Every organisation has undiscovered gems waiting to be developed
11. Removing the barriers to pride of workmanship and joy of learning unlocks the true untapped potential of the organisation

Figure 9.2.

Here, the combined set of beliefs, values, and management principles is refreshingly and practically different. Many schools might even find it difficult to grasp what this school is trying to say. It is what is absent from this set of beliefs that is so strangely important. No overt mention is made of teaching and learning or quality as such, and yet this is exactly what this set of management principles is all about. What Mount Edgecumbe School has done is set out the kind of conditions needed to create a system that allows students and teachers to function effectively.

This school is saying confidently that the world of relationships inside and near to the school is what will make it a great school. It demands a complete and coherent system in which everything works and makes sense. If something goes wrong, it is first a systems issue not necessarily somebody's fault. Its considerable strength is that managers manage the system so that everyone can work with *joy*. They do not manage people because they fear people will mess up.

What this school is also saying, is that to be successful, continuously improve, and have great outcomes requires that relationships within the operational learning system work effectively and with quality built in. Relationships are first on the list, and it is these that underpin learning. These beliefs ensure that the school is constantly examining what works and what to do when things do not work. In effect, it is in command of common cause variation, and this dissipates the unpredictable nature of special cause variation. It creates a school where double-loop thinking constantly informs the learning process despite not mentioning learning once.

Such a useful ideology stems directly from the fourteen points set out by Deming (1986) in *Out of the Crisis*.

THE MOUNT EDGECUMBE WAY

To write this school's management beliefs, the leadership of the school has clearly studied management theory and practice and especially the work of Deming. They studied practical management not visionary leadership. The latter grows out of the former, inside-out, not outside-in the heady way Western culture understands and promotes leadership and the right to lead!

Ah! You might say. The schools is still a factory school because although as a system it now works well, the learning is still not what is needed for the twenty-first century and there are still time limitations and variation difficulties. True, and the school's context is different to most; but this working strategy is part of the change process needed to create the basis for a better approach to learning. It is a big step toward autonomy and independent thinking and systems thinking like autonomy!

Learning Relationships Rule OK

In all of my work with hundreds of schools, virtually every single principal spoke of the importance of relationships between staff and students, and yet every single one operated a system that made such relationships difficult to build and maintain despite such good intentions. Their frustration was always the same: *we know we can do better but there seems to be something wrong and we do not understand what it is. There has to be a better way.*

In Mount Edgecumbe School, the managers manage the operational learning system to ensure that mess ups are minimized and this is what's different. In the West, school leaders follow a variety of inadequate leadership programs that are increasingly *command and control* in nature, and these are simply not the same thing at all. We seem to be fixated on alignment to growing lists of so-called leadership personality traits, somehow *knowing who we are at 360 degrees* (if that is remotely possible) rather than understanding the systems that others must operate and work. With more management knowledge and a bit less introspection, there is a far greater chance of being a good leader.

The belief system of this Alaskan school is entirely different to most and which tend to be aspirational and loaded with assumptions. Too often, belief in parent partnership is simply vacuous, and contains no reference as to how the operations within the school as an organization actually make such a belief real in any customer care sense. For Edgecumbe, beliefs and management actions must be complementary and synchronized, otherwise neither has any impact. It is this absence of management knowledge in US schools, the home of modern management, which causes schools to rely on old hand-me-down assumptions and a set of beliefs that no longer have any real meaning. It is a training issue. For Edgecumbe, the three Cs are vital system components: customer, culture, and capacity for continuous improvement.

These simple remedies start to create a fully interconnected and nested learning support system. As the system builds, transformation of every facet of school life must follow, and this means sufficient unlearning to ensure old ideas are abandoned. Otherwise, the constant barrage of add-ons, fixes, regulations, and policies is making it impossible to see the forest for the trees as Sherwood (2002) suggests. In our schools, children have just a few set years to be measured and graded. It is a heartbreaking teacher-dependent race with few winners. Many students are robbed of the time they need to reveal the talents they have and many may never show what they could do and could be.

For a school to be truly effective, teaching is not enough. It requires effective tutoring and mentoring, and it is this that is missing from most schools and certainly those with horizontal, un-nested structures. To be effective, parents also need the tutor more than ever. This may seem a romantic systems thinking view, but then the common sense of interconnectivity is like that; it has a metaphorical and metaphysical compatibility but is still essentially a practical and common sense approach to management.

Looking at schools as systems, parents still have trust and still harbor their dream that the school can help them and involve them. I have never met a parent who did not want their child to do well at school—not one. Neither have I met a parent who did not want at least someone in the school who knew their child well, someone they could talk to who would always be there. Schools need to respond better to these aspirations and can do so despite suffering the ideological systemic distortions of trust exercised daily by centralist *reformers* who should know better.

Ludwig von Bertalanffy reminds us of the unique potential of all of our kids, their open and active personality systems, and gives us every reason to strive for a better, more joined-up world. He has given us a beginning point and a spiritual end point to better schools. The school system can have a means and a purpose, and with a little redesigning and thought, can realize so much more because of the teachers we have, not despite them.

Urie Bronfenbrenner has given us what systems thinking always gives: a clear picture of what is needed and how things can go awry, why so many active personalities have gone under and continue to do so, and why teachers have wrongly been apportioned blame. But he gives so much more. He offers clues about what schools need to do and be to avoid damage to the fragile bio-ecological microsystem of a child's learning relationships with adults and other students. We can go a long way to healing our schools so that they work better for kids and families, and we can do this at no cost as we build our systems thinking school!

So, now we have the beginning and end and the start of the middle needed to construct a better strategy for school improvement. We can think about what a school needs to do to operate as an effective, organic learning system. We need schools to be able to fix most things themselves, and we need to somehow do it before children and teachers are exposed to even more defeat in our broken factory schools.

Deming always proposed that the people doing the job are the best people to do the job and so should be able to make the changes that make work work better. Our schools are packed to the gunnels with talented people (young and old); all they need is a little light learning to apply the systems thinking needed to release their creativity. In using the work of systems thinkers, the contributions from other psychologists have not been ignored. Systems thinking is embracing. It is, as defined previously, a mode of thinking that recognizes the requirements of learning relationships and operational processes in a practical and common sense way.

In this respect, the overarching bio-ecological system model can be reasonably said to incorporate Erik Erikson's psychosocial ideas from analytical psychology as interpreted by Richard Stevens (1983). It has no problems combining with Jean Piaget's stages of cognitive development or Abraham Maslow's (1943) theory of motivation. It seems to fit well with John Bowlby's (1969) attachment theory, which highlights the important role of caregivers in child development. The same can be said of Albert Bandura's (1977) role-modeling and with Lev Vygotsky's (1978) sociocultural theory, where once again we are reminded of the crucial role of primary care.

STORIES

In many ways, psychology uses systems thinking to map out stages and feedback mechanisms that create the scaffold needed to understand ourselves. Mention has not been made of Sigmund Freud. I simply refer you to Lucy Wadham's wonderful book, *The Secret Life of France* (2009), for an insightful account of the French education system and of the philosophy and psychology that holds sway there.

I discuss these stories to show how the technological age with its changes to work patterns and reliance on devices can interfere with family systems as Bronfenbrenner suggests. Where interference is high, as in the United States, there seems to be a loss of personal engagement and time, and this is likely to affect learning and challenge teachers. It is difficult to teach people who are looking at their smart phone or who are texting beneath a desk.

At dinner and other family times, I have become acutely aware that I am the only one who has not parked a smart phone next to my dinner plate and that I am alone in not texting or dealing with calls as though they were some part of the dinner conversation. This is not only because I am incompetent and still completely unable to use a smart phone, or because I have no friends, I just think it is rude and resent the way technology invades family life at almost every level. It is as if I am intruding by being at home! Bronfenbrenner and others such as Sherry Turkle (2011) in her book, *Alone Together: Why We Expect More from Technology and Less from Each Other*, are right to draw this to our attention. Vertical Tutoring (VT) acts to rebalance such an invasive trend.

My wife is French. She despairs of the behavior of groups of French kids let loose around London by their teachers. Patricia would prefer to live in New York and I in France, but then I am more sanguine. I raise this because technology appears to be causing a crisis in parenting in the United States as Bronfenbrenner suggests. France is at least resisting as best it can.

Pamela Druckerman, in her book *Bringing Up Bébé: One American Mother Discovers the Wisdom of French Parenting* (2012), says children should say *hello*, *goodbye*, *thank you*, and *please* because it helps them learn that they are not the only ones with feelings and needs. In her book, Druckerman views French kids as being calmer, better at meal times, more civilized, cheerful, chatty, and optimistic. She notes that in years of watching French kids in playgrounds she has never seen a temper tantrum except from her own child! When she asked French parents about discipline, parents interpreted this as meaning *education*.

Personally I also find French kids and families generally more pleasant to be around than those in the United Kingdom and the United States. I too find French kids are more helpful, more family orientated, more socialized, and just more *on message* and that all of this is because of parenting values and traditions that have not been overly buffeted by technological change and the use of new technology. Talking is just about winning over texting.

French culture is still clinging on despite the losing fight to retain its essential Frenchness. For me, buying a baguette in a small boulangerie starts a day of conversations and life-affirming smiles and mini-relationships far away from the factory anonymity of the supermarket. Schools should take note. Judith Warner (2005) is well placed to pass comment. Her book, *Perfect Madness*, follows a similar theme.

For her, middle-class US parents in what she describes as *an Age of Anxiety*, try to ensure that their children's wants and needs come first, no matter what. In the United States this is called "advocating for your child and is . . . predicated on the belief that if you didn't yourself do it, didn't teach your child to 'self-advocate', no one would, and in the great stampede for resources and rewards your child would get left behind in the dust." Some might call this another *tragedy of the commons.*

As a dad and a former school principal, being in a position to semi-embarrass kids has always been a dubious pastime. We all notice at school parent evenings the space many children like to keep between themselves and their *embarrassing* parents. So, whenever I gave a school assembly and especially before summer break, I would tell the students (ages 11–18) "Don't forget . . . make sure you go for a family walk; be safe and hold hands when you cross the road; and always kiss your parents goodbye. . . . And be back on time. And remember to say *please* and *thank you.*" This is all in preference to a text message asking to be picked up from somewhere two towns away.

The students and staff used to laugh at this *uncool* and childish absurdity. Over time, however, all I had to say at the finish of an assembly was, "Don't forget . . . ," and they would then finish my assembly sentence, having heard it so many times. Often, when some of the older students gave an assembly to their peers or to younger students, they would get back at me by ending their student assembly using the same words albeit in part mockery of the boss. But to my amazement, many parents and students commented on this and some noted that there was a change in their children. It had an effect. Bandura would have been proud of me!

Teachers learn as much if not more from the kids as the kids do from teachers. School is a world of stories, surprises, learning, and the gossip that holds people together—social interconnectivity. What I learned was that learning relationships precede learning programs, not the other way round. The former enable the latter; it is a case of distinguishing common cause variation from special cause variation all over again, but psychologically.

The inspiration for that assembly was not really mine. In an article for *Readers Digest*, "We Learned It All in Kindergarten," Robert Fulghum (1987) wrote of the importance of sharing, playing fair, putting things back where you found them, washing your hands before you eat, drawing, singing, dancing, and playing and working every day. "And it is still true, no matter how old you are, when you go out into the world, it's best to hold hands and stick together."

So, what of the school's sense of purpose? That purpose is to grow the child into the best person that child is capable of being in the world we have, no matter how long it takes. Works for me!

Fulghum reminds us that what is really important is really simple.

Chapter Ten

Mixed-Age Mentoring

Human beings of all ages are happiest and able to deploy their talents to best advantage when they are confident that, standing behind them, there are one or more trusted persons who will come to their aid should difficulties arise.
—John Bowlby, 1969

The extraordinary way out of the wicked problems schools face is to abandon the linear industrial model of school organization by introducing a vertical dimension as the leverage needed for the school's cultural transformation necessary to promote better teaching and learning. This also means reconsidering the age split between middle and high schools and looking at alternative models that allow for a greater age range, say 11 to 18 or grades 6 to 12. There are still one classroom schools in the United States and many other countries that have such a mix, and where students help each other. In such places the teacher *facilitates* learning and tends not to be such a dominating factor.

In 1987, a study took place that had the potential to revolutionize school organizations, but the opportunity passed by. It is time to look again at this area because VT as a systems thinking change takes mentoring and learning relationships to new levels. The concern then was as it is now; the call for reform amid worries about US competitiveness (National Commission on Excellence in Education, 1983; Task Force on Education and Economic Growth, 1983). It was thought that technology, computer-assisted instruction (CAI) would provide an answer. Henry Levin and colleagues (1987) conducted an investigation at the middle-school level.

They effectively posed this question: Given one hundred dollars per student for each of the subjects, mathematics and reading, which would be the most cost-effective given the choices of (a) increasing instruction time, (b) reducing a range of class sizes, (c) using CAI, and (d) cross-age tutoring?

Peer tutoring came out on top. Had the study understood VT as a system, the cost effectiveness would almost certainly have been considerably higher given there are no real costs involved as such! Further, students acting as mentors enjoy a considerable gain in their own learning.

When we look at mixed-age mentoring systems, especially in the United States, they tend to be adult-led. In fact, in the United States, the education system goes to extraordinary lengths to prepare and professionalize mentoring, usually for *wayward* students. The main thrust is, as ever, reactive: downstream rather than upstream. In this section, we need to think about the child not only as a recipient of learning but also as a leader of learning, and this means *every* child in the school acting as a young teacher, leader, or mentor, not just the selected few. It makes systems sense.

In horizontal systems the person who learns most is the teacher, so if all the kids teach, they should learn more, and strange as it may seem, there is increasing evidence that they do just that, given the chance (Ehly and Larsen 1980).

This helps widen our view of teaching and learning beyond the classroom to build a whole-school learning process to which everyone contributes and everyone gains. This requires a look at mentoring as a key component of the school's learning armory and of the development of pro-social, more empathetic attitudes. There are at least a half-dozen or so other powerful combinations and sources of learning and learning support beyond the classroom, many of which are diminished or absent in linear systems. Of course, schools claim that all are thriving and in place, but this is not true and neither is it managerially possible in horizontal structures.

These sources of mentoring and learning support include:

1. The child as a learner being mentored by another student.
2. The child learning with peers and mixed-age groups as a supportive team.
3. The tutor intervening and working with a student on specific areas that could include behavior interventions.
4. The tutor engaging an older student to mentor and support learning for a mentee in tutor or home-group time on a specific subject.
5. The parent(s) or family supporting learning in liaison with the tutor and teacher(s).
6. The tutor and parent engaging with a child to review and agree on strategies for improvement (forty-minute academic tutorial or learning conversation).
7. The tutor and teacher agreeing on a strategy with and for a student.

There are many other supports, such as community work, work experience, external advisers, extracurricular activities, and assemblies, in which learning takes place. The organizational challenge for schools is to tap into these resource riches to enable learning and to keep it switched on. However, these combinations of learning relationships have a further advantage; they can be easily connected and six of the seven outlined occur in school. When looking at schools, it is important to see a more complete picture of learning as a whole-school process that links the school to more of itself and to home and the world beyond.

Such a full double-learning loop, which includes teaching and learning in the classroom, relies on a multi-nodal information flow among all players. This means that input from teachers, tutor, home, and child is needed to create an effective operational learning and support process, and this requires all key adults to tend to this learning loop continuously. Such a process must also include the development of pro-social behaviors within a full consideration of the needs of each individual student. It sounds complicated, but all that is needed is the vertical design enabler.

All of these characters and the tasks they undertake depend on information flow, and this too requires review and change to ensure understanding and effective application. Learning information must extend beyond target and assessment grades to strategies for improvement, attitudes, and behaviors to be truly useful in supporting and managing student learning. The ability of the tutor to orchestrate and manage the interconnectivity and mentorial support needed completely changes the way a school approaches and identifies management tasks—an internal systemic change.

Only when this is all in place, and the common cause variation issue is addressed, is it possible for another important piece of the learning jigsaw to work much more effectively:

8. The teacher and pupil learning relationship in the classroom.

Schools actually operate the wrong way around! They start at Point 8 where it can take considerable time to build learning relationships and reciprocity and then have to work systemically backward to plug learning gaps—or try to—because of the weak assumptions schools hold about learning values, priorities, and psychology—confusion about what is effective and what is not. At the risk of repetition, the teacher is dependent on the first six learning relationships being organizationally operational and in place *before* the student even enters the classroom. Only then is the teacher able to access and use a complete learning support strategy (learning process), and be confident about the back-up for what he or she is trying to do and be.

Once in place, children entering the classroom are at far less risk of failing in learning or becoming victims of negative social experiences (prey to negative in-group loyalty). It is the tutor, not the teacher, who is the key go-between charged with building new loyalty groups within tutor time, and this is the key to raising the self-esteem that builds the confidence that enables leadership and gives the child sufficient ownership to fan any small flame of aspiration.

The teacher's own proficiency level also has a chance of being significantly increased through the school's information and support, communication network, and in particular by the work of the child's tutor. The learning relationships formed in tutor time between tutors and tutees and older and younger students affect confidence, attitude, reciprocity, and enables leadership. These qualities can transfer to the classroom situation because all players are process-involved and understand how the new learning system works. Such a simple system is based on real behaviors involving trust and individual responsibility, not lengthy policy documents. The teacher no longer has to battle for control and fret about isolation, and the child no longer has to give up the fight to be heard.

Instead of the homeroom tutor being potentially the weakest link in the learning system, the new interconnections make the tutor the potent force that connects people and learning. The management teams must now learn to focus on how such a network is best supported in both time allocation and information richness. Managers should now manage the system first.

MENTORING AND LEADERSHIP

Margaret Wheatley (2004) observed that leadership should appear everywhere in an organization, wherever it is needed. If leadership is to appear everywhere, this poses a challenge in our schools because this is not what we have. To have leadership everywhere is not a viable proposition in linear models strangled by policy, procedures, and time constraints; for leadership to be everywhere, all children must develop leadership skills and be given leadership responsibilities. To achieve this, mentoring has to be introduced as an embryonic model of leadership. We need tutors to mentor their tutees and older children to mentor younger ones and peers to feel confident mentoring peers.

Schools also need to involve parents in a world where parenting is less than easy. Leadership is not the distribution of power to the chosen few as some suggest; neither is it a restricted and precious commodity. It is an innate talent that can be revealed in myriad circumstances. The challenge is to develop within the school's normal operational learning process, a means whereby every single child is both a learner and a teacher—what might be termed a mentor and mentee learning capability.

While the idea of the school student mentor is widespread, it appears almost entirely as an undeveloped add-on for those young people considered *damaged*, and this limitation is a result of linear thinking. It tends to be used only when a child is seen as failing or deficient in some way. In our schools, there are usually a few older student mentors who may play a bit part in helping out. Otherwise, in the United States, the many schemes in operation usually comprise volunteer adults dealing with *problem* kids, the usual reactive approach that comes too late for the dropout.

The best way forward is to look at models to see how they work and find evidence of this happening. Remember, every child a learner, every child a leader, and every child a mentor every day: the whole operational child learning system. All of these mini-system entities are almost by definition vertical or cross-age. It is also stuff that children do all the time, part of what it is to learn, empathize, care, show consideration, and grow up. Some call this *family*.

MENTORING PROGRAMS

Perhaps the most recent example of wide-scale mentoring is the research project led by Peter Tymms (2011) of Durham University that involved seven thousand children from 129 primary schools (under age eleven) in Scotland. From the before- and after-assessments, his team concluded that when children helped other children learn, there was a consistently positive effect. He also suggested that at this stage of schooling, cross-age tutoring with a two-year age difference secured the most positive results. At the secondary level, there is greater age flexibility and similar gains reported by schools that fully embrace VT.

Tymms also noted that when a child teaches another child there is a double or wash-back effect. The teacher child or mentor also learns at a deeper level. This knock-on effect is also recognized for its many positive benefits in those schools trained in VT. The student mentors make additional personal gains in self-esteem and learning confidence, which they take to the classroom, making the teaching job more open to taking creative risks and more fun.

Student mentors are trained, given responsibility, and trusted, and this strengthens their own openness to learning and especially to a more intrinsic approach to learning that can come from improved levels of self-esteem. But there are other important pro-social and pro-learning benefits. Whenever one child helps another, the school facilitates a *learning relationship* between two young people and initiates positive in-group loyalty. When one student works with another in a clear and purposeful way, this is, in effect, another kind of positive behavioral intervention.

Not only is active and personalized learning more likely, but there is also positive intervention in any negative in-group loyalty as a new positive pro-social group is born, and these possibilities are seemingly endless. Such whole-school mentoring opportunities offer the possibility of new relationships, positive attitudes, and better behaviors forming as new loyalty groups grow around the child replacing negative ones. This student activity can be summed up as follows:

1. When student mentees are supported by student mentors up close and personal, it increases interpersonal knowledge and understanding (empathy in part) in addition to raising confidence in learning. When at the same time children are trusted as mentors and trained to lead and support, there is a resultant increase in self-esteem and an immediate intrinsic learning and knock-on classroom effect (providing schools understand how to managerially construct the process mechanisms in play). The potential for teaching and learning to advance is then better facilitated: confidence leads to a willingness to take risks and the classroom teacher and learners all benefit.

2. When the tutor is given a mixed-age tutor group, the school has a system potential and capability in place that can readily lend itself to developing a deep and more consistent range of strong pro-social behaviors. This also means that the homeroom tutor or vertical form tutor is better able to be the person he or she needs to be, developing a range of learning relationships between parents, staff, and children, all with considerable spin-off advantages. The tutor becomes the consummate advocate, mentor, and guide by the side rather than the sage on the stage, enabling quality to be built into learning relationships that does not have to be won solely in the classroom. Even adult tutor self-esteem and confidence increases, and this too is taken to the classroom.

3. The learning system becomes increasingly active, supported, and integrated across the whole school in increasingly effective and joined-up ways. Instead of operating on 30-percent efficiency (classroom alone), the school is using all teaching and support personnel in a more proactive way. Systems management is redesigned to suit the mentoring facility by organizing the complete learning system around the tutor's role as the communication conduit and as performance director. The twenty minutes of tutor time per day, when mixed-aged kids meet up as a tutor group, becomes organizationally vital to all parties.

In VT schools (i.e., schools based on an appreciation that there is a shared responsibility for building the learning process centered on mixed-age tutor groups) interventions in reading are particularly powerful. Older students are able to deliver reading programs to complement specialist intervention and so prevent children being withdrawn from lessons. Although the kick-back is always improved learning confidence and greater and self-esteem, it also results in building empathy, a more caring society, greater openness to life-long learning, and more successful outcomes.

The main point is this: Schools tend to approach what they call peer mentoring in an ad hoc or superficial way, whereas Tymms's research rightly suggests that a more systematic approach would accrue greater benefits. When such a system is in place, the teacher and student in the classroom are immediately connected to all other support arrangements (i.e., tutor, mentor, parent).

The important systems thinking learning points should be kept simple. In so doing, a successful school mentoring scheme should:

1. Allow all children to be mentees, mentors, and leaders—everyone a teacher and learner.
2. Ensure training is integrated into the whole learning process, including for student mentors.
3. Be evaluated so that everyone can share the success and improve the design.
4. Encourage the purposeful development of learning relationships (positive in-group loyalty).
5. Be understood as a means of handling demand and variation issues while minimizing failure.
6. Be integral to the whole-school teaching and learning process to improve all outcomes.

Schools can then start assessing and reporting in a more balanced and holistic way to parents and internally to each other, perhaps appreciating that although parents send schools a *whole child personality system*, schools simply send back a set of grades, the miserly bits that schools and kids are now measured by.

These characteristics treat mentoring as a key school activity in which all are involved and not as an add-on. With this process in place, other systems thinking design issues arise. Much greater consideration is needed for assessment and reporting, management and leadership, and changes to policies and practices. Horizontal systems fail in part because (a) most of the students are not personally challenged and offered real responsibilities, (b) tutors and parents are unable to access critical information at critical times, (c) intervention is slow and inadequate, (d) the communication network is weak and malformed, and (e) the quality of customer information is limited, restricted, and generally poor.

Mentoring must be process-integrated and never be an add-on. When learning relationships are properly established, they can replace or enhance many other pro-social programs, and in this respect citizenship, tolerance, diversity, and community cohesion all start to make sense, opening the possibility for greater success when specialist programs are needed. What is the point of offering a taught citizenship program if the child is overwhelmed by the realities outside of school? By practicing citizenship in tutor time in real time, the taught program makes more sense and has more chance of working.

The rule is, learning relationships before learning programs, always!

MENTORING IN THE UNITED STATES AND THE UNITED KINGDOM

The United Kingdom has one system advantage over the United States: a long history of houses and tutors. Historically, the English House System was the platform for in-group loyalty and leadership and being a member of the House was all important, as Harry Potter and his chums knew well. Similarly, being a House Captain or House Master or Mistress was a job of great importance. The system is still strong in UK independent schools. This concept has been diluted and almost abandoned as a working organizational ethic in the UK education system and been replaced by a year system.

There are two matters to note. The adoption of same-age tutoring or the unfortunately named *homeroom* (US) has actually undermined and badly diminished the role of the tutor if not quite destroyed it. It has done this by separating homeroom tutors from their real purpose so they are unable to function properly and cannot deliver on their own job description, a quite bizarre piece of management.

The second matter concerns school types. In the United Kingdom we have seen middle schools (equivalent of junior highs) come and go—mainly go. In the United States it seems that little thought has been given to ages and to schools. If learning relationships are to form and if they are to have some permanence, the less a child has to change schools the better, especially at critical learning times. The distinction between middle schools and high schools requires reconsideration and a degree of reunification. There are massive two-way advantages to having great role models around for younger students.

Mentoring in the United States tends to follow what researchers often describe as *damage models* targeted at socio-psychological development (Townsel 1997). Others involve information or counseling support to improve learning or to advise on matters, such as careers. In the main, those students regarded as at-risk are the key beneficiaries, despite *all* kids needing help at various times. Linear schools tend toward this kind of model mainly because of structural limitations of what can be achieved.

Beyond this, research comes thick and fast and with the research comes a lengthy catalogue of suggested criteria, techniques, safeguards, conditions, specifications, targets, and more—certainly enough to make any school think twice before committing to new ideas. In this respect, what should be fairly straightforward systems thinking in school can too often become bureaucratized, expensive, and complex.

Dubois and colleagues (1997, 2002) at least bring back some sanity and advocate parental involvement; otherwise it is clear that mentoring is unnecessarily seen as carrying its own daunting limitations and leadership challenges with it. Despite difficulties of context and management, Rockwell (1997) gets to the heart of what is needed and helpfully suggests that schools should be viewed as *mentor-rich* environments. These are places where teachers and tutors are "known, trusted, available, informed, and already committed to the well-being of youth." These mentor-rich environments could be enhanced through

> small learning communities or schools-within-schools that might facilitate closer working relationships; encourage more complete understanding among teachers, students, parents, and community; foster a sense of belonging through multi-year teaching, school clubs, and projects; and promote feelings of ownership through more individualized instruction.

This is a fair description of VT as a system and like Bronfenbrenner, Rockwell provides further input for the design blueprint of the systems thinking school. The idea of leadership and mentoring everywhere and nested systems of schools within schools is reflected in Rockwell's vision. Of course, teachers cannot do this alone, but developing an organizational systems thinking process that embraces mentoring is achievable and simple to do when the approach is multiyear (vertically based) as Rockwell suggests. Homeroom or tutor time twenty minutes per day five times a week would do this nicely and with room to spare.

Rockwell has all but described the attributes of a systems thinking school with its essential vertical dimension. In Rockwell's model, not only is leadership available wherever and whenever needed, but mentoring is also. There are conclusions to be drawn:

1. When a child enters a school, responsibility for learning is a shared process, and there are many learning relationships that need to be enabled. System management and design must reflect this.
2. When these new partnerships work, it is possible to see a whole child developing and not see a child as just a set of grades. This enables support and intervention.
3. Recognizing the complete child will lead to better outcomes and well-being.

4. A return to growing great people is more likely to grow a better school and a better country. It might also jumpstart a better paradigm, creating an improving ecological fit.
5. Teaching and learning improves when learning relationships are designed in, and do not have to be won and formed solely in, the classroom.
6. Families are important and need recognition as does the student's voice.

THE SCHOOL AS A COMPLEX ADAPTIVE SYSTEM

On July 8, 2012, I spent the morning watching the Olympic Triathlon in Hyde Park, London. That same evening, I watched as Great Britain's cycling team picked up more gold medals. As someone who once played sports you learn the meaning of being part of a team, of working to a common purpose, of knowing the job you have to do, of the power of in-group loyalty, and of the heightened sense of being alive that being part of something beyond yourself can bring. Every single gold medalist interviewed throughout the Olympics thanked their parents first and then their team of coaches, their PE teachers, their school, the medics, and mechanics that supported them: team gold for team people.

Dave Brailsford, the track cycling performance director and mastermind behind Team Great Britain's cycling prowess, was asked the secret of their success. His answer was succinct: it was all about the *aggregation of marginal gains.* Everyone has to know their job within the improvement process and everyone has to work together toward a common goal and see the big picture. Every detail counts. The job involves thinking about a complete interconnected system. What does the cyclist need to achieve more, to be the best they can be?

So, the question is how to make these significant marginal gains; by what method? It is not possible to instruct and manage marginal gains just as a system cannot understand itself as Deming said in his system of profound knowledge. Marginal gains derive from the release of creativity, from working with complexity, from communicating and sharing ideas, seeing things differently, looking at the most complete picture and drawing knowledge from other disciplines. This might involve the swapping of ideas via myriad wild feedback loops, looking at other systems but always thinking of the rider and the bike and the coaches and the mechanics as a complete system brought together for a purpose. Eventually a bunch of neural impulses power down a different synaptic pathway and a new idea forms. What if . . . ?

The learning system that seeks such gains is never there to be tamed but to be allowed to *emerge* into something more than it was, what it was meant to be. The more tight and loose teams that work on the challenge, the more opportunity exists for information to be better used and for creativity to be released; it is in essence the problem-solving idea of the knowledge society. Team Child is no different. Other students, parents, tutors, and teachers all have to gather knowledge, including input from the tutee, to make the marginal gains that might make all the difference at graduation.

As purposeful and often seemingly disparate teams form and reform, a process called *emergence* occurs. The group, team, or system takes on a life of its own; it starts to *self-organize* and explore its environment, driven more by subjective intuitions and intrinsic drivers rather than the current school fad of action research alone; it begins to look beyond itself at other possibilities, at other disciplines, and other thinking. It can start to learn, and this means it can adapt and evolve.

Roger Lewin (2001) describes such a process in *Complexity, Life at the Edge of Chaos*. Instead of managing complexity and trying to reduce variation, self-organization embraces complexity; it needs complexity to seek out the best solutions. Complexity cannot be simply wished away. We need to recognize that schools need to be more complex not less, and that we need our children to be complex because both increase creative opportunities to create something better, perhaps increase the commons. All of this poses problems for managers. As Lewin says,

> Where managers once operated with a machine model of the world, which was predicated on linear thinking, control and predictability, they now find themselves struggling with something more organic and non-linear where limited control and a restricted ability to predict are the norm.

A child mentors another child in a school in tutor time. Now multiply that across thousands of interactions in a school and observe the release of an astonishing degree of leadership, support, generosity, and creativity. This is complexity and this cannot be managed using linear management methods; it has to be released. To better understand an organization like a school, it is best to see it as a *complex adaptive system*. The sorry alternative is to view a school as a simple factory system wherein human variation is discounted and reduced to a manageable one-size-fits-all norm. David Shenk (2010) warns us that the methods we currently use may well be denying the genius that we need.

Each model has a different relationship to complexity. Each can improve standards. But the non-linear model is able to create and work with complexity to aggregate gains without resorting to expediency and the accumulation of expensive waste; it is more at ease with diversity as possibilities for improvement, creating and revealing value and good.

A complex adaptive system cannot be linear and mechanistic; rather it is one that is complexity dependent but still able to create flow and feed on the communication and interactions that constantly form and reform (open, double-learning loops). Lewin would describe a school more easily as a biological system, one that is constantly evolving, removing from it as much mechanistic human thinking as possible. Schools lead and need a metaphorical and metaphysical life, and this means managing differently.

Meredith Belbin (1996) set out the key features of future organizations with two management principles and a model that explained why ants appear to be so much smarter than humans in managing and embracing complexity. The model, adapted here, is as follows (with the addition of a School column).

Belbin suggests there are two management principles to emerge:

- There are better ways of running a complex organization than by making it the responsibility of the single boss.
- The larger the body corporate, the more important becomes the need for an organization to be built around concurrent systems, differentiated in terms of function and scope, but interlinked rather than separated.

ORGANIZATION	HUMAN	INSECTS	SCHOOL
Nature of Hierarchy	Centralization: individuals oversee and over-rule.	Devolved nature of operations. Some hold more vital jobs than others.	From centralist to devolved. Everyone understands their role and how the system works to support learning.
Social Behavior	Emphasis on individual gain.	Focus is on the needs within and of the colony/community.	Focus on every child as a whole person using all resources.
Communications	Top down: command and control; restricted. Junk material at other levels.	Lateral, elaborate, and multi-nodal. Full interconnectivity.	Fully interconnected and orchestrated via the front-office tutor. Combines vertical and horizontal channels.
Speed of Response	Delays due to single channel upward referral and to intricate appeals systems in public sector.	Rapid reaction force operating locally and containing all the necessary specialisms. Leadership and mentoring everywhere.	Leadership and mentoring everywhere. Customer care and service a priority.
Source of Specialized Services	Extended education and training. Aptitude obscured by formal qualifications.	Castes with genetically appropriate behavior. Conversion of castes to meet perceived needs of any situation.	Tutor able to draw down resources as needed. System built around tutor as the catalyst for learning.

Figure 10.1.

Ants are particularly good at building systems. However, both the human model and the ant model are run by junkies. The human one is run by power junkies and the insect one by chemical junkies. Yet, the ant colony is far more successful because every ant knows what it is doing and (let us pretend) why it is doing what it does (purpose). We need our schools to be learning organizations able to grasp all that complexity and diversity has to offer by applying systems thinking principles. As Lewin suggests, the solutions we need to manage adaptive complex organizations are more likely to be found in a biology that is other than human!

Every child and every tutor is different, every group different, every family different. As Deming so often intimated, variation is everywhere, which is why we should do more to appreciate both its complexities and its management. If we over-organize tutor time into delivering pro-social programs or instruction, which is what command and control organizations do, and demand that tutors account for every minute of time, this becomes waste of a high order created in the name of order.

Donella Meadows (1991) described why it is better to have numerous contact nodes: "A diverse system with multiple pathways and redundancies is more stable and less vulnerable to external shock than a uniform system with little diversity." Such a system is also likely to enable people to work better and achieve excellence and quality in what they do as well as create a higher probability of innovation and ecological adaptation.

Finally, they say that sports build character, but this is not quite true. Sports *reveal* character just as schools should *reveal* talent, as David Shenk suggests. The teacher is part of a team and so is the parent, the child's personal tutors, and the child's mentors. They contribute their ideas and expertise to make the significant marginal gains needed, but it is the vertical tutor that makes it all work. The vertical tutor operating from the home room and the tutor room, is the performance director, sometimes hands-on, mostly hands off. All that schools have to do is set up a process and the training that releases the tutor's capabilities to make it all work.

The real message of mixed-aged tutoring and mentoring is clear. It is powerful and should involve all kids at all critical times and as many informal times as possible. All kids can teach, all kids can lead, and all will benefit from a helping hand when needed; support everywhere, leadership everywhere, self-emergence everywhere with high expectations of each other. The VT systems thinking school is built on this premise.

Chapter Eleven

What Schools Say: Lessons for Managers

The small piece of research set out herein began in 2005 and has continued to the present day (first set out in *Vertical Tutoring*). Over the years, this ad-hoc research has involved between twenty-five and thirty thousand people, mainly teachers, support staff, and governors working in UK secondary schools but including China, Germany, and Qatar. The most important factor connecting all of the 350-plus schools involved was their adherence to a year system of organization.

The people in the study were all members of schools requesting information and training in VT and systems thinking; they all shared a belief about the importance of relationships in their school, and their passion for schooling, though bruised, was undiminished. All wanted to be better even though some were already recognized as high-performing schools. The leadership teams of the secondary schools involved all believed that the year system they were using to manage their school was not working as it should and, despite many attempts at changing their approach, it remained stubbornly ineffective, unwieldy, and damaging.

THE SURVEY AND RESEARCH

The question posed during training was this: Who has the most influence on a child's learning (positive and negative combined) out of teachers, parents, tutors, and peers? It's a simple enough question. Teachers and support staff and school co-workers were asked to self-divide into small groups and rank these players in order of influence, then apply a percentage score. The group time given was five minutes.

Regardless of the type of school and the age range, the results from each school remained remarkably consistent. I still conduct this survey today when working with schools and still the results remain strikingly similar regardless of whether the school is 11 to 16, 11 to 18, single-sex, a faith school, or whatever.

The results are as follows:

Choice	Rank Order: Who has the most Influence on learning +/- combined (horizontal system)	Influence on Learning %
Family	1	35/45%
Peers	2	30/40%
Teachers	3	15%
Tutors	4	5%

Figure 11.1.

This small chart tells a small story about schools operating on horizontal systems and contains much information to inform managers and leaders. From a systems thinking point of view, these common-sense indicators tell school managers that to run a school effectively, they need to work more closely and intensely with families than they have ever done before, given that they believe families wield so much influence. This belief says that Urie Bronfenbrenner's third proposition, which stresses the importance of parents and teachers working together, needs close attention. Similarly, if peer groups have a powerful and sometimes negative influence on the learning of others, then the school must understand how in-group loyalty systems operate at peer level and how best to intervene effectively to ensure that a student's aspiration gene remains switched to the "on" position. It has already been stressed that such interventions cannot be achieved using pro-social educational programs alone but is made possible by using new and positive mixed-age loyalty groups to build resistance to negative anti-learning pressures.

The intervention has to involve mixed-age groups, given that large, same-age peer groups are managerially unpredictable and unwieldy, and herein is another paradox concerning complexity. Peer group complexity is deep seated and often difficult to dissolve. Mixing kids into multi-age groups is more complex but is far more open to adult leadership and far easier to work with, given knowledge and a little training.

Participants in the survey clearly said that in linear schools with same-age groups, the tutors' influence on student learning was very low (rarely above 5 percent). This is the complete opposite of what they would assume and expect, given management expectations and the tutors' grandiose job profiles. Teachers as ever were hypercritical of their own influence and placed themselves third, at 15 percent effective with regard to learning. Parents and peers were the highest by far, with parents just winning out over peer groups, although it was never unusual to sometimes see peer groups occupy first place in this survey of secondary schools.

A number of general observations could be drawn when these results were further investigated during training.

1. A high proportion of tutors felt undervalued, ineffective, and uncertain about their tutoring role in a year-based peer system. Leadership teams (LTs) harbored many concerns about the quality of their tutor teams and their effectiveness. They blamed tutors for being ineffective rather than an ineffective system. This concern raised doubts with LTs regarding a move from a year system to a vertical culture and what they perceived as a more sophisticated and tutor-dependent system that required higher tutor skill effectiveness. Members of LTs often expressed concerns during LT training that their professional staff team might not be capable of meeting the demands of a vertical tutoring system.

2. The reason given by LTs for low tutor effectiveness was tutor quality (echoes of teacher quality) not system management and the broken linear learning process. In part this was because all schools had tried a wide variety of methods and reforms (that word again) to improve tutor time or home time with limited success. Managers simply lacked the systems thinking skills needed to find their way out of this predicament and failed completely to understand that the horizontal system in play conspired to undermine hope of tutor and tutee learning relationships forming.

3. The family is seen as the most important influence on learning, but none of the schools remotely appreciated or understood parent *partnership* in terms of building customer relations and managing student diversity beyond an offer of subject evenings, PTAs, and letters of information. Schools now text message parents and allow them access to assessment data, something many parents resent because of the lack of personal contact. Schools keep reinventing information systems (one-way) rather than communications systems (two-way).

4. The criteria for customer care set out herein are anathema to schools. Despite all that schools do to promote what they perceive to be parent partnership, it remains minimalistic and bound by perceived and confused requirements on union working time directives and fear of mistakes. Parents are generally supportive of schools but too willing to accept the vagaries of their partnership with the school as normal.

Communication is largely absent; information is restricted and minimalistic.

5. Teachers undervalue their impact and feel less influential and effective than they might. They are aware that they are perceived as a *quality problem*. Teachers did not appreciate that there was a direct systems link between their performance as teachers (15 percent) and their self-perception as tutors (5 percent effective) and the subsequent quality of teaching and learning in the classroom, despite most holding down both roles.

6. This last point is critical. Staff undermined in one area, as tutors in the homeroom or tutor room, are immediately damaged as effective teachers in the classroom and so is student openness to learning. The learning relationships in tutor time fail to form and go to the classroom in a state of disrepair.

7. According to those who work in schools, peer groups in horizontal systems have a powerful influence on the learning of others—and not always a positive influence! Such influence groups are particularly challenging. The school's horizontal organizational culture makes these highly effective and resistant social peer networks even stronger, and these can give rise to challenging and unpredictable behaviors and attitudes to learning. Where there is separation between home and school (weak partnership) peer influence can more easily occupy the vacant middle ground, adding conflicting information to the home–school relationship.

From a systems thinking point of view, a school's intention to promote quality in learning must understand the current system process in play and action system change. These powerful influences on learning do not go away, so the task of the systems thinking school is to ensure intervention and management strategies that promote a positive contribution from all parties and, critically, to understand how these learning and communications loops might be best achieved. In this respect, there are several points to consider that might help create a different systems approach to schools and inform how schools might be better managed:

- If parents and peers are so influential, these are the people with whom schools need to engage at a deeper partnership level than is the case. This is especially so at each stage of schooling, such as at entry, pre-exams, at feedback and reporting times, prior to course selection, and at other critical learning times. These are occasions when learning is most vulnerable and learning partnerships, support, and intervention are most needed. In fact, these times are priorities in the school's academic calendar. The key partnerships or learning relationships within a child's bio-ecological sphere must be in place in a way that is as predictable and permanent as possible. Such matters cannot be left to chance, allowed to drift, or be assumed in any way.

- The status and role of the child's tutor must be reinstated and revived. The child's homeroom tutor is best placed to engage with parents, students, and teachers by establishing the school front office, customer focused, communication, and support conduit. The logistics have to make sense. To do this first requires an understanding of how the tutor role in horizontal year systems came to be marginalized, undermined, and diminished to avoid repeating such system management and design errors.

- When linear schools kill the tutor, they badly injure the teacher, neglect the child, and damage parenting. Any systems thinking school must redesign the networked school learning system around the tutor to connect child, parent, and teacher with learning. This allows for rapid intervention and prevents schools from becoming part of the eco-technology that damages families.

- If peer groups are such an influence, greater thought must be given to successful in-group intervention techniques that prevent children from dropping out and failing. This is critically so on the first day of school, before a child even enters the teaching classroom. The tutor-child relationship must be established quickly and before any so-called team-building exercises, circle times, and group getting-to-know-you games occur. Systems thinking must show how this can only be done in a vertical tutor system: relationships must be started, albeit embryonic, in tutor time before the child is exposed to taught programs if these are then to make sense.

- Teachers do what they always do, which is to give their best effort. When things go wrong, they look around at their isolated position within their departmental silo. Too readily, they unwittingly accept all responsibility because they have been allowed to become the totality of the learning system of the school. School managers and leaders who are now encouraged to build the organization around their function almost without reference to how the school operates elsewhere. This is industrial design at work, but it is the direction schools too often take.

If tutors see themselves as unimportant and impotent at the same time, as the survey suggests, the school can never work as it should and teaching and learning suffer accordingly. There is a double whammy! If the tutors rate themselves at 5 percent effective or less and they take that 5-percent feeling of ineffectiveness and low self-esteem to the classroom where they teach, the teacher's confidence takes the hit. This creates a potentially toxic classroom situation. If kids take their negative in-group loyalty to the classroom without previous and appropriate intervention, the teacher faces a mountain of potential resistance, allowing only the most outstanding teachers to survive.

The challenge to schools is to enable the form tutor to be that magnificent person working at the front line of the school just as schools declare in their literature and as set out in the tutor's job description. At every turn, however, what a school says and what a school does turns out to be a compromise in quality and a failure of management and, therefore, leadership.

EXTENDING CUSTOMER CARE

The school as an organization is constantly engaged with three challenges: the amount and nature of variation the system has to handle, identifying and securing the value work for the customer, and ensuring ongoing quality to meet environmental and contextual demand. Although a systems thinking school is able to endorse these three ideas and recognize all participants (i.e., student, parents, and school) as service providers and service receivers, the linear model faces inescapable restrictions. But it also faces cultural barriers of long-cherished separation between players. Schools have never really seen the need to involve what many see as *interfering* and *meddlesome* parents.

The key component parts of customer care at the home and school level (Johnston and Clark 2001) might be adapted for schools as follows:

- **Communication:** The extent to which there is a two- and three-way (i.e., parent, tutor, tutee) dialogue between home and school; the ability to listen, analyze, and agree on strategies for improvement and support learning and learning outcomes.
- **Trust:** The degree to which the school or the home partner depends on the work or recommendations of the other without seeking extra justification or collaboration. In some cases one partner may commit the other to work without prior consultation.
- **Intimacy:** The process of sharing important information for the benefit of the learner, thus removing barriers to learning through close partnership and support strategies.
- **Rules:** A mutual acceptance of how this particular relationship operates: what is acceptable and desirable and what is not.

Schools just do rules! Rules are needed to compensate for the distortions created by common cause variation. The greater the complexity, the more rules, procedures, policies, and practices are needed. The essence of customer care requires fewer rules and more flexible and interconnected systems. As a child progresses through school, the need to share more complex information increases substantially. Parents need schools, schools need parents, and kids need both to be operating on the same plane(t). Sadly, the home-school *partnership* that began reasonably well at the gates in primary school starts to drift slowly apart at the secondary school, just at the time of maximum need and when thoughts about dropping out are starting to form.

In a complex organization like a school, not only does everybody supply and receive services but the success of the organization also depends on how those services flow. The organization has to be both totally interconnected but must also be able to increase quality. The system has to enable all students to mentor fellow students, tutors to advise teachers on changes, tutors and parents to be in touch as needed, teachers to advise tutors on a student's performance, and so the communication system builds in a way that communication, trust, intimacy, and rules become endemic, a part of the culture.

Such a massive increase in track requires a system that is able to flow.

THE EMERGENT SCHOOL

It is now possible to complete the model of the systems thinking school. It is one that all schools will know and one that schools may wrongly assume is already in place. To the previous systems thinking model, the student as mentor has now been added. The working model must be stable and flexible enough to allow information to *flow* around the system to invigorate and support system players and inform and modify the learning and teaching process. The tutor has to be the system conduit, orchestrating what is needed and how information should flow.

This model recognizes that all parties must contribute to successful outcomes. Metaphorically, it is a journey through time that requires home, school, and child to work together, but a journey that gives the child the confidence and abilities to explore alone. All the child needs to know is that he is safe and that nothing can go wrong. Maslow (1954) saw this as a journey that required an ordered approach wherein motivation required fulfillment and attention to basic needs to reach higher levels such as self-actualization. The systems thinking school subscribes to such an approach. For learning, the goal is to become an intrinsic learner and any systemic change should seek to do just that.

The higher the quality of information, the more the system is informed and able to respond quickly.

This model enables strong Team Child cohesion and the kind of self-organization that ensures ongoing stability and maximum predictability. In such a system, common cause deviation is more easily understood and controlled, leaving any cases of special cause variation exposed and, therefore, more quickly and easily managed.

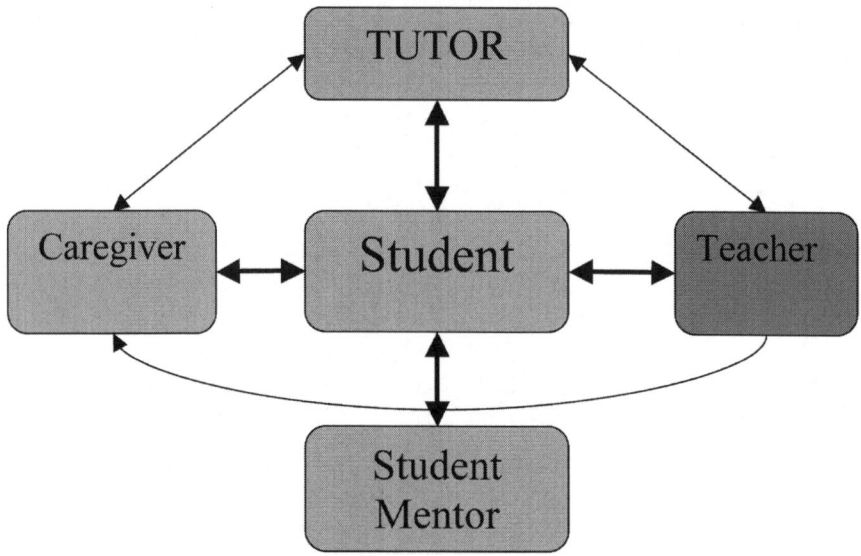

Figure 11.2.

SYSTEMS THEORY AND MANAGING CHANGE

Systems theory is very much about eliminating waste and concentrating on delivering value to the customer. Waste in school linear systems is organizationally generated by the need for repeat work, failure in upstream learning, insufficient systems knowledge, managing people rather than the organization, annual performance reviews, not understanding what is of value from the customers' perspective, mistakes, failing to communicate effectively, minimizing information, and the list goes on. The waste, if not removed, restricts flow and this leads to negative demand (complaints and repeat work), and so the organization starts to fold in on itself and become moribund.

The vertical dimension frees schools by rectifying how the value stream operates as an interconnected communication system dependent on the free flow of information and the capacity for rapid intervention and support in the learning process.

It should be no surprise that schools tend either to resist change or go about change led only by vision and a limited range of management skills. School managers are high-order people, and it is not their fault that they spend so much time doing wasteful things; it is a training issue born of institutional inertia. Although there is no shortage of vision in most schools, it is unlikely that a revised VT vision is enough to change such a situation, given an absence of systems thinking knowledge and systems understanding. Even when schools try and change from one culture to another, schools employ old managerial approaches and invariably take orthodoxy with them as an unneeded passenger. Nevis and colleagues (1996) put it this way:

> To transform something is to change its fundamental external form or inner nature. . . . In the world of nature, a caterpillar is transformed into a butterfly; its DNA remains unchanged, but its form and properties are fundamentally different. A butterfly is not a caterpillar with wings strapped on its back.

Having worked on VT as a system for cultural change for many years, you gain an appreciation of how the butterfly emerges. There are strict requirements, adherence to values and management principles; understanding and seeing the big learning picture is essential. Unless the value stream works effectively, all players are prevented from being the people they are meant to be. Any deviation from the inherent values and management principles, or adaptation to orthodox ways is a risk. Schools often "go vertical" without any appreciation of the need for unlearning or of the values and principles of management required. They simply strap wings on the school caterpillar, just as Nevis suggested, and there is no transformation.

John Kotter's Eight Factors Affecting the Success or Failure of Transformational Change	
Doing these things increases the probability of creating successful transformation	**Doing these things decreases the probability of creating successful transformation**
Develop a sense of urgency	Failure to develop a sense of urgency; as in, "Let's take things slowly."
Establish a guiding coalition	Failure to establish a guiding coalition; as in, "We can do this without help."
Develop vision and strategy	Failure to develop vision and strategy; as in, "We don't need a new vision—our old one is just fine."
Communicate the vision	Failure to communicate the vision; as in, "Why do we have to talk about this, everyone knows what it is?"
Empower a broad base of people to take action	Failure to empower a broad base of people to take action; as in, "We don't need those people to help us. All they'll do is slow us down."
Generate short-term wins	Failure to generate short-term wins; as in, "Let's not worry about early success—let's keep our eye on the long-term goal."
Consolidate gains and produce more change	Failure to consolidate gains and produce more change; as in, "Wow, we did good. We don't need to do any more and we don't need to toot our own horns."
Institutionalize new approaches in the culture	Failure to institutionalize new approaches in the culture; as in, "Well, we made all these changes. Now we can sit back and relax and not worry about making sure they are working properly."

Figure 11.3.

Frank Duffy (2007a) is right to make constant reference to the challenges faced by any transformation together with the paradoxes that block the pathways. In particular, he refers to John Kotter's (1996) table of factors likely to affect the chances of successful transformation. These matters form the battleground where old culture battles with new concepts, where leadership comes into its own to do battle with paradoxes.

One of the many interesting insights that Kotter raises is that single-loop thinking and special cause variation (right-hand column) dominate the linear management culture. Double-loop transformational learning (left-hand column), seeks to engage with system change and tackle any common cause variation issues. Transformation requires deep cultural change to attitudes and a willingness to unlearn long held practices that have dulled vision; these are not easy matters for schools. Until we get school managers to engage in a more precise vocabulary based on better systems knowledge, systemic change will continue to be hindered.

To repeat Michael Fullan's (2008) comment, "Perhaps the best way to view leadership is as a task of architecting organizational systems, teams, and cultures—as establishing the conditions and preconditions for others to succeed."

The imperative of *lean* is to stay *authentic*. This is defined by Deborah King (2002) as "the everyday acts of people who take responsibility for improving teaching and learning in the entire school community." Similarly George Cappannelli and Sedena Cappannelli (2004) suggest that *organizational authenticity* is the systemic coherence of core mission and ethics. This should make systems thinking and lean thinking coworkers because both adhere to being authentic.

Behind systemic change is a major training issue for our schools, and considerable thought is needed on the timing and content of such a major undertaking. What is clear is that the repair and reform training now in play falls short in too many ways. Vision is not simply the prerogative of schools as organizations but, more importantly, of those that seek systemic change. The challenge is how to align schools with systemic vision and purpose in a way that better informs the vision of school leaders. Vision and training can no longer be seen as separate during transformation.

In this respect, Louise Stoll and colleagues (2006), in their literature review, state that

> International evidence suggests that educational reform's progress depends on teachers' individual and collective capacity and its link with school-wide capacity for promoting pupils' learning. Building capacity is therefore critical. Capacity is a complex blend of motivation, skill, positive learning, organizational conditions and culture, and infrastructure of support. Put together, it gives individuals, groups, whole school communities and school systems the power to get involved in and sustain learning over time.

Chapter Twelve

Building the Systems Thinking School

> The companies that survive longest are the ones that work out what they uniquely can give to the world not just growth or money but their excellence, their respect for others, or their ability to make people happy. Some call those things a soul.
>
> —Charles Handy, 1997

For Charles Handy (1997), leadership is that odd combination of passion, risk, drive, and doubt. It is neither teachable nor learnable, but more a matter of the right individual finding his or her passion in the right circumstances. A systems thinking school should always invite such passion. In Handy's view, school should be split in half, with the morning devoted to a learning core and the afternoon devoted to an individual or personalized curriculum, tailored so that kids leave school with a portfolio of competencies. These demands are part of what is spurring system change; customers are demanding more music, more creativity, more engaging science or, at the very least, that their child be taught a common core.

Schools are being pushed increasingly by customer forces into becoming places in which every child is treated as an individual and in which learning is far more bespoke and individualized. All of this points to a different view of what constitutes a values stream and customer care; more flexible, college-style schools will surely follow. Handy once asked the question, "Why would you want to devote your life to an organization that can't give something special to the world?" We need to transform our schools to being those places that give something special to those who walk their corridors and to the commons generally.

That said, the systems check is over, and there is now sufficient knowledge to look at some of the practicalities needed for transforming the culture of the school in preparation for full systemic change. We can then test what has been built by looking briefly at assessment for learning (AfL) to see if what has been created within the vertical structure does what it claims and is of the quality needed. We should expect to see a complete double and triple communications loop linking the classroom to the tutor room to the home and back again as a continuous and coherent dialogue.

What follows applies to all schools, but what I have in mind is a secondary, a middle school or high school. It does not really matter. We shall knock over barriers and barge through the paradoxes as they present themselves.

In a horizontal or year-based school, the homeroom or form tutor has notional oversight of the learning and development of around 25-plus young people of the same age, usually throughout their time in school. The form tutor may not actually teach the same young people in his or her care and does not need to, but usually spends a short time with their homeroom group covering registration, administration, supervision, and occasionally some content areas.

FROM THE HORIZONTAL TO THE VERTICAL

The systems thinking school must fully embrace the culture that VT jump-starts with an initial investment of about twenty minutes per day. When the implications of VT are understood, this small time allocation starts a domino effect that builds a new and more complete learning process to which all facets of school life become geared. It is able to affect a complete cultural change to the school's end-to-end operational learning and teaching methodology impacting positively on demand and variation issues: it will drive improvement to learning and teaching faster than anything else a school can do, eventually inspiring innovation in learning and teaching.

To make this change, the horizontal tutor or homeroom tutor must become a vertical tutor and work with children of all ages in the twenty minutes of tutor time. In making this change, it is vital that the school manages such a change using systems management principles and values (which are set out herein) rather than logistics alone. Do-it-yourself efforts based on what Shukla called *arrogance and ignorance* or simply copying other schools leads to critical mistakes and a rapid return to industrial management ideas. During this role transfer from a back office-dominated system to a front office system, the management culture of the school must transform and evolve to suit the new model.

Instead of trying to build a school around the classroom as a component, it enables the classroom by viewing learning and teaching as a system-wide process involving everyone, and this is the fundamental and operational system shift in thinking. It is a shift from back-office delays and process errors to front-office information flow, customer care, and rapid intervention.

The vertical tutor group is a mixed-age group of young people brought together on the basis of balance (gender, abilities, intelligence(s), ethnicity, etc.) but not friendship. In effect, this is the first direct intervention in the powerful peer-based in-group loyalties and in any broken family values; this happens before the child enters the secondary classroom. In this way, it is preparatory to teaching. In other words, any induction to a school that a child receives has to be carefully choreographed so that tutor and tutee meet in a close-up and informed way to maximize the construction of the school's first learning relationship. David Hargreaves (2006) refers to this kind of working and mentoring relationship as *co-construction*.

The next people that any school newcomer will meet are some of the student's older classmates with the tutor briefly in attendance.

Set out here is the order for managing change.

PREPARATION AND TRAINING: ADOPTING THE NEW PHILOSOPHY

The transformation much begins with Deming's (1982) second point, *adopt the new philosophy*. This means understanding exactly why the linear structure fails as a learning system in order to grasp the systems thinking approach that the change to VT requires. This is also the point where organizational change is most likely to go wrong and wings most likely to be stuck onto caterpillars. The school leadership team has to be the first to understand the concept of VT at a secure, systems thinking level if successful implementation is to be achieved.

Once VT is understood as a systems thinking strategy at a theoretical level, it is possible to think more about implementation at a practical level. Set out here is how it is best approached, starting with a radical review of tutor-to-tutee ratios and how tutors are selected. These ideas are based on intensive work with more than four hundred secondary schools.

Every year, schools decide their home-room or tutor teams. Most staff are exempt because they are regarded as too important or too busy; the job has little status, little effect, and a limited purpose if tutor and student perceptions are anything to go by. This commitment is about twenty minutes per day minimum and around twenty-five minutes maximum!

BUILDING THE COUNTERINTUITIVE FOUNDATIONS

In 1909, the first junior high school (Indianola) was born in Columbia, Ohio. Since then, secondary public schools in the United States have been broken in two: middle school and high school. Middle schools provided what many saw as an early twentieth-century answer to a failing system, one that tallied with the new psychology of the time. What seemed an obvious and logical division, however, is entirely industrial and out of sync with modern context and ecology. It is in fact, another remnant of common cause variation linked with linear thinking; the author appreciates that many will find this view unpalatable and hard to accept. People are incredibly protective toward schools.

Since then the elementary (five grades)-middle (three grades)-high school (four grades) split has taken root (Lounsbury 2009). Like horizontal systems, a whole research mythology is built around this component part of public education. It seems such a neat idea, breaking down learning into some kind of assumed psychological fit. Besides, some argue, it protects younger ones from the dangers of the older ones! VT argues the complete opposite, and on all fronts. The need to change school simply does not stack up as a viable system or make learning and learning relationship sense. The big overall system is failing and this means confronting much that is assumed, which includes the strange junction box of middle schools. We need to be counter-intuitive.

This book has no intention of promoting a systems thinking school that depends entirely on undoing what cannot be easily undone. It has to work with what there is. The fact is that middle schools bloomed and have now largely died out in the United Kingdom and most are glad to see the back of them. It is this that has allowed diverse and more systems thinking schools and ideas to grow. In the United States, the systems thinking school must work with a broken system, and though not ideal, VT can work in middle and high schools. It would simply work so much better if middles and highs were combined.

At this point, we are dumping the name *home group* (home is where the child lives) and simply referring to *tutor groups* or even *student bases*. If the school is to respond to demand and be able to manage the huge social and learning variation it faces, consideration must be given as to how quality can be built in and time might be better managed. The tutor has to be retrieved from the *problem pile* and be seen as the solution to organizational challenges.

It starts with a simple long division quotient. Calculators ready?

The aim is to seek an optimal size of the VT group, that is, reduce the size of the tutor groups to secure a better opportunity for building a new web of learning relationships based on positive in-group loyalty and psychological need. This should be around twenty students per group, smaller if possible. The aim is to make all tutor groups about the same size. Within the tutor group, the number of children from a given grade (ideally) should not exceed four.

Figure 12.1.

This number is not arbitrary; it is one that optimally lessens the risk of unwanted cliques forming while maximizing opportunities for student leadership, responsibility, and mentoring. Nothing should stand in the way of developing leadership and the task of working toward more intrinsic motivation. In essence, instead of a large and powerful peer-based in-group loyalty arrangement, the school creates smaller, familial and supportive vertical in-group loyalty that is far more effective in neutralizing bullying and gang membership, while better promoting the idea that it is cool to learn. If meeting the tutor is a first intervention in negative in-group loyalty, the vertical composition of groups and the influence of older students is the second.

People often worry that many older students are the problem with schools, that children need protection from them. The counterintuitive truth is that when students are trained, have a supportive and reciprocal relationship with adults, are trusted and given responsibility, they are simply amazing with younger students given the chance. They become the role models younger students need and older students want to be, something almost entirely denied in linear models.

How these groups are built, formed, and led is what matters and is one of the keys to a school's vertical tutoring success. The tutor's learning relationship with the child must be established on entry to the school and with the rest of the tutor group if the teacher and child learning relationship is to flourish and not be compromised or delayed. On entry, the first thing that must happen is that the child meets his tutors (there should, if possible, be two). The child then meets a few older children who will guide him or her that first day and in the days that follow, all under the tutors' supervision. These short meetings are essential. The child cannot simply be sent to the classroom with insufficient back-up. The tutor wants to know how that first day went as much as parents, and so, too, do the older students.

The tutors have, of course, prepared for that meeting by looking at data and files and discussing how best to approach that first interaction. If the tutor is successful in building, supporting, and sustaining positive learning relationship (care) there is a higher chance of classroom transfer and of success (every child mattering, no child left behind, and every child leading and learning). I'll try and make sense of this as we proceed. Suffice it to say that although tutors are also teachers, their success as teachers is linked inextricably to their success as tutors in the joined-up way that systems thinking principles demand.

FORMING THE VERTICAL TUTOR GROUPS

Having established an optimum tutor group size based on values and management principles, the horizontal (peer-based) tutor groups have to be undone and reformed. This starts with two more interventionist strategies. The first ensures that young people who influence each other negatively are in different VT groups. The second ensures that friendship is not a factor in forming the new tutor groups. This reduces the formation of unwanted cliques while maximizing the opportunity for forming positive in-group loyalty, successful intervention, and learning support. It also introduces the child to the working notion of teams and especially the mixed-age mentoring and leadership teams most likely to benefit everyone in so many ways.

The object is to create balanced tutor groups based on factors such as gender, ability, need, and ethnicity so that all groups share a commonality of form. Just as the family is a form of school, so the tutor group becomes a form of family in terms of its learning relationships. It is important to bear in mind that a child learns much from the way a school is run (Sizer, 1984) and much from social modeling behavior (Bandura 1977).

Listening respectfully and carefully to a child is also a modeling of behavior just as much as teaching, explaining, forgiving, admitting fallibility, and so forth. Both open the way for how tutor time might be effectively used. There has to be a safe place in the school day beyond the classroom and away from the power of the peer playground where at least two key adults (each group has two tutors) are always on hand to facilitate pro-social behavior, sound psychological development and joint nurturing of a child's ecosystem just as Urie Bronfenbrenner suggests. Learning and achievement are under constant scrutiny and enjoy constant support and rapid intervention.

Tutor time is dynamic in this sense. The effective involvement of older children as *assistant tutors* is important, and these leaders or mentors not only promote trust but also a sense of citizenship and what it is to be caring, empathetic, and supportive. Social learning programs can never do this as effectively; it requires the purposeful and carefully planned formation of mixed-age groups to enable such qualities to be released. In this way, the programs make more sense but are needed less! Once the tutor groups are formed and are functioning, formal pro-social programs should be far more effective but will require more sophisticated design.

Tutors do not deliver such programs in a formal sense. Their role is to create learning relationships that enable the children to benefit from their need for more information and so increase their human capabilities. Remember, this activity in tutor time is the key to the full learning system. The learning relationship always precedes formal learning very much in the way that Abraham Maslow's *Pyramid of Needs* (1954) sets out a rationale for growth and self-actualization. Each pyramidal step depends on the previous step. Once the learning relationship is in place and things are safe, the child can take learning risks knowing the tutor and older students have his or her back and nothing can go wrong.

All staff members should be involved in forming the vertical groups. The first compositional draft of the new tutor groups is developed by a team that knows the students well. All staff are invited to comment on group composition to inform further changes until a consensus is achieved on the make-up of the VT groups. New friendships come later and old friendships are maintained. It should be noted that students may not like the idea of shifting from familiar friendships to new ones over which they have no choice. They too, have to understand what VT is and what's in it for them and consultation with parents and students (not choice) is important!

SELECTING AND ALLOCATING THE VERTICAL TUTORS

Having indicated the vital role of the tutor and having compiled the new tutor group lists, we can now allocate the tutors to the tutor groups; again, management principles and values come into play. This is still a paper exercise. No one has met anyone else yet. The tutor we have in mind is beautifully and simply set out by Alfie Kohn (1999): "In order to be a caring person, a parent or teacher must first be a person." This is fortunate because schools are full of *persons*, many of whom are prevented from being persons and rendered dysfunctional in the schools we too often have.

There are hundreds of schools where senior staff have told me that they could not possibly increase the number of tutors by a third, which is what VT demands, because they regarded the existing standard of tutors and of tutoring as too low (in their horizontal system). They claim not to have sufficient staff of sufficient quality. Ironically, the reason schools hold this view relates to the school's failure to see the system damage done to their tutors instigated by very same management team that complains about them! It is just as Robert Trivers said (2011)!

Only after training and *unlearning* do they see that the tutor is not such a hopeless case but is a person who has been completely undermined by the broken system in play, one that renders the tutor ineffective and wrongly maligned. To do a decent job (tutoring) there has to be a decent job to do other than child minding, taking attendance, giving out notices, and teaching programs that are inappropriate and that can never properly work or be managed. But these are the kinds of management distortions schools have operated for years, and the damage to learning and to teaching standards has been considerable.

To counteract this, a lead tutor is allocated to each tutor group and that lead tutor is selected from *everybody employed in the school regardless of their status*. This must include senior managers. However, even this is insufficient for the tutor task, and there are many highly capable people who work in our schools who will be anxious (after training) not to be left out. These might include library staff, security staff, technicians, counselors, support staff, etc.). To each tutor group *we* add a co-tutor to complete the tutor team. If necessary, we can make up the numbers with volunteer parents.

As a school principal, I was also a vertical tutor, albeit an average one, and so was my personal assistant, the school secretaries, the librarian, and all teaching assistants. They were comparatively brilliant and probably remain so. At parent consultation evenings on VT, parents sometimes remain behind to say that they too would like to contribute by being co-tutors. This is a wonderful opportunity for a school and, if carefully managed, enhances VT. It sits the school deep in its community.

The school must now adopt a new employment policy based on the value that the school places on high-quality tutoring: no adult should ever be allowed to join the school in any capacity without understanding that he or she will be *expected* and *trained* to be a lead tutor or co-tutor with joint oversight of a group of mixed-age children. Almost everyone employed by the school should be a tutor; this engages everyone in the central learning purposes and operational process of the school. These people are the lynch-pins of the interconnectivity with parents, teachers, tutors, and children; the accessible and quality communication and information dialogue needed to support people and learning. This is a whole-school conversation.

Young people are much more likely to grow into caring adults if they themselves are cared for in a real sense. A key purpose of a school is to develop pro-social values, responsibility, and an active notion of citizenship. Creating the optimum conditions for these qualities to develop without resorting to social programs alone is essential in any systems thinking school. VT depends on this personal, principled, dynamic, and values-driven approach that cherishes ideas of self-organization and emergence and that can master the challenges posed by variation.

In the systems thinking school, we have started to create a new operational end-to-end learning system by establishing the fundamental framework and process for building a whole set of interconnected learning relationships across the school and with parents. This extends beyond the subject classroom but remains connected directly to it. During tutor time there is the chance to intervene positively in in-group loyalty and to create close learning relationship and support opportunities (what Jonathan Haidt [2006] might call the *inbetween*).

So far we have expanded the number of tutor groups in our school and dramatically reduced the tutor-to-tutee ratio from 1:25-plus to 2:18/20. Almost all school staff are now linked to the school's operational learning support process, a major investment in intrinsic motivation and support. Within the school, we are starting to build a nested system of mini-schools and within the mini-schools cross-age groups and subgroups, schools within schools, can be formed.

Kohn (1999) quoted a text from staff at the child development project in Oakland, California. Their purpose was to find a means of helping kids become more caring and responsible. Of course, in the absence of VT and full-scale mentoring and tutoring, they came up with a program. The philosophy of that program mirrors the role of the tutor group and it is this that is of interest here. To internalize pro-social well-being and embark on a moral journey, children should be helped to be part of a caring community.

Their description of community is precisely what a tutor group is in a VT school. It is a place

> where care and trust are emphasised . . . where each person is asked, helped and inspired to live up to such ideals as kindness, fairness and responsibility . . ., a . . . community that seeks to meet each student's need to feel competent, connected to others and autonomous. . . . Students are not only exposed to basic human values, they also have many opportunities to think about, discuss and act on those values gaining experiences that promote empathy and understanding of others.

Kids do not need a diet of change programs, ten-point plans to a better life, our endless toolboxes; they need the opportunity to be part of an optimal and supportive group that best enables them to grow well and to learn. The difference is that the vertical tutor's approach is largely program-free. Program dependency is a US weakness and is based upon false assumptions: programs have a place but most are a substitute for real learning, an idea rather than a reality. Schools can do better. It is all too easy to become hooked on them as a reform solution.

The idea of programs as therapy for system conditions wrongly created simply returns to the teacher's door as waste. The answer is not a better program to improve pro-social relationships; it is in fact not teaching social programs until pro-social relationships have been formed and can be continually supported. When a child leaves the classroom, the influence of the taught social program is exposed and easily overwhelmed by massive media and peer group pressures. Programs are all too easily forgotten and rendered insipid in their power to intervene, to heal, and to guide those perceived to be most in need of them. To be effective, they have to be socially joined up to the rest of the school and preferably replaced by tutors and mentors.

Otherwise, tutor time is played out in real life with real consequences and with friendships and relationships based on high values such as trust, responsibility, and permanence. It cannot be that we have to build a system so dependent on outstanding teachers and seemingly compliant children. We need our schools to be places where every teacher and school worker and parent can contribute and be valued, including ordinary ones like me. It is ironic that in the West we are blessed with the best teachers by far but operate the most confused learning systems.

All that needs to happen now is for the two tutors to meet their tutees.

THE TUTORS AND THE TUTEES

The question is this: how do the tutors and tutees meet for the first time? The students have all been allocated to different mixed-age groups and probably do not know each other. They will be a little nervous about the new arrangements. There is a whole set of learning relationships and new friendships about to form and the school needs to get this right. To accomplish this, the previous strategies used by schools have to be abandoned. These tend to be class-based getting-to-know-you activities and team-building activities—the flotsam of the failed horizontal system. Schools are repeat offenders but insist that what they do works. They are so wrong.

The first meeting, when tutors and mixed-age tutees meet for the first time, requires a different and far more personal approach. First, they must unlearn the wrong way, the way that ignores psychological need and is high risk and loaded with assumptions about what schools think should happen. What untrained schools do is arrange some kind of VT "launch day." They organize a special day almost identical to the horizontalist's induction day. There are team-building exercises, getting-to-know-you activities, problem solving, and the like. The assumption is that everyone gets to know each other, including the tutor, and lives happily ever after within the new vertical cooperative.

What actually happens on such launch days is something different and less obvious. In-group loyalty marches on unchecked and there is no successful planned intervention by the tutor. Children learn their in-group pecking order. It is all hit-and-miss and largely assumed. It is a day that will never be repeated, an add-on when the key relationship between tutor and tutee is assumed to somehow embed. It is a repeat of the horizontal school induction day, the time when children join the school on day one. What may seem fun and worthwhile can actually undermine teaching and learning; risk-laden launch days do the same by demeaning the tutor's effectiveness and preventing relationships forming while assuming they do.

So, how should the tutor meet his or her tutees for first time? Best practice requires some preparation and a deeper understanding of what a systems thinking school is trying to achieve. There are three areas of preparation:

1. The first involves a training and preparation session for older students in mentoring and leadership. We can legitimately call this a training session because we need all of our senior students to be prepared for their part in VT as lead members of the tutoring team. This only happens at the start of VT before implementation. From then on the students learn from practical experience in tutor time.
2. The second is to create information sessions for tutors to sit down and go through the files of their tutees. This includes meeting with other staff as necessary to learn more about each student before actually meeting them, to get that first handle. This also unites the tutors and their purpose as strategies begin to form regarding student needs.
3. The third is to ensure that parents and students are aware of each step along the way. Parents or caregivers will meet the tutor later, soon after the term has gotten underway.

The first meetings between tutor and tutees must be short, more intimate and focused. The approach is unexpected. Tutors should *not* meet children in vertical mixed-age groups initially but in their horizontal year or grade groups of four students for around ten minutes. So the first contact is two tutors (lead and co-tutor) engaging with up to four same-age students.

The tutors do most of the talking in this occasion: they talk about their role, VT, expectations, and how it all works as a learning and support system. They become a *person*. It is a brief but focused encounter about expectation, responsibility, and trust, and the purpose is to begin the process of forming new loyalty groups with the students and between students. The tutors are really announcing that they will always be there, predictable and dependable, monitoring, supporting, mentoring, and guiding. The tutors will also announce that they will be the key liaison with parents and teachers.

It is a conversation (albeit mainly one-way) about care, expectations, support for learning, the future, a picture of VT, and learning relationships. It is an offer of leadership and trust to the students and is the start of raising the self-esteem and confidence that will transfer to the classroom and beyond. For students it will be their first school conversation of this kind, but it will be the first of many as speakers and listeners learn to interchange roles. Such a meeting should start with a warm handshake to signify that this agreement of mutual support is different, important, and permanent.

This small meeting is repeated for each year group (grade) over a week before implementation at the start of the next term or semester until the tutors have met all of their tutees in this personal way. In those meetings, new combinations of positive in-group loyalty start to form rapidly, reflecting the care taken by the school in getting the process and the teams right. There is no need to meet as a full vertical group at this stage, and any attempt to rush things and over-organize kids in the way schools are driven to do should be avoided.

We are in the summer term: it is July. VT starts in September and at that time older ones and younger ones will meet each other for the first time. That too requires care and is set out below (Day 1 of VT).

TUTOR TIME

For decades it has been customary for children to enter school in the morning and spend time being registered for attendance. In the horizontal systems children too often see tutor time as an opportunity to be tardy: *It's only tutor time; we can be a bit late*! *It's only tutor time!* To place tutor time at the beginning of the day, at the end of the day, or before and after lunch is poor management, which confuses what is important with what is convenient and again undermines the tutor and the teacher while sacrificing what is of value.

To be valued, tutor time should be placed in a slot before morning break. This has a number of advantages. Not only do young people of all ages go to break together, but this time slot also provides an opportunity for the tutor to have that quiet word besides providing a longer break in the day.

PARENTS

At the upstream end, parents have been waiting patiently for a systems think-ing school that acknowledges that they not only exist but are an integral part of the school's learning process. In the term before implementation, they are invited to an evening where the benefits of VT are set out. It was explained by the school principal that

> VT is all about working more closely with parents than before, improving student outcomes through higher quality communications, ensuring rapid intervention, knowing every child well, making sure all students feel supported and monitored, and improving learning and teaching. In effect, parents are being given what they have always wanted; someone at the school who knows their child well that they (parents and child) can talk to.

The new partnership is described. It is fairly easy for the principal to set out a host of reasons for going vertical and all are ultimately concerned with im-proving student outcomes and well-being. Usually, there are only two con-cerns that parents have. The first is a worry expressed by their child about splitting up friendship groups and the second is what parents perceive as the potentially damaging effect of older children negatively influencing younger ones by exposing them to unsuitable behaviors.

The short answers are simple. A child spends twenty minutes a day in the vertical tutor group, a small proportion of time away from same-age friends. There is no friendship loss but there is a significant friendship gain. And what about the dangers posed by older students? The feedback from the hundreds of schools that have adopted VT (even the ones that have got it wrong) is that bullying is reduced significantly as are suspensions from school. Behavior and attitudes get better not worse, and younger children actually feel safer and more comfortable than before when they have older children with them. Why should we be surprised? It is classic counterintuitive reasoning. Tutor time is a time to practice leadership, build self-esteem, be listened to, and be made accountable.

If establishing key relationships is the first stage of creating a systems thinking school, the second is building in the changes needed for systems management, and that means changing the way things are traditionally done. This includes time management, assessment, report sequencing, scheduling, and even most school policies. All require attention and development as the system builds. Although changing the relationships is revolution in terms of pace, the rest is evolution but rapid evolution guided by new priorities, principles, and values. The procedures used to manage the industrial, linear model are not the same as those needed for a vertical and systems thinking school.

THE BASIC MANAGEMENT MODEL OF A LARGE SYSTEMS THINKING VERTICAL TUTORING SCHOOL

The basic design must reflect the interconnected learning loops that link all key players (i.e., parents, students, tutors, and tutees). Rather than the split hierarchies of *care* and *curriculum* of the old system, these are integrated within the tutor's front-office responsibilities. The school is divided into a small number of houses or colleges according to size, preferably an even number of houses containing a mixed cohort of students (age and gender). Heads of houses should be regarded as school principals in their approach. Although they each run a house, they should work from the same shared office to ensure a collegiate approach, exchanging ideas and managing systems development. They work to ensure that the system operates creatively and effectively with fun!

The tutor group resembles Bronfenbrenner's nested model and the child's bio-ecological system. The whole is orchestrated by the tutor, often working through tutees and student mentors. This comprises a whole series of positive loyalty groups constantly interacting, all interconnected. The smallest unit is two people, then three or four, then the whole group—all counter negative in-group loyalty and foster interventions and pro-social behaviors. The group is guided by the school's academic calendar so attention is given to those who need it.

Surely, some may argue, given that the tutor knows the child so well, the tutor is best placed to deliver pro-social programs. The counterintuitive argument holds good. This is the last thing tutors should be asked to do. Excellent tutors do not make excellent deliverers of programs, ever! That is a specialist job. Put simply, tutors do *not* teach programs; they monitor, support, lead, advocate, reciprocate, intervene, liaise, take a deep interest, draw down resources, redefine what it is to care, contact parents, talk to teachers, examine data, and promote learning without fear. That is enough!

They ensure that every child is deeply known by at least two people in the school who are passionate about what they do and who they are. They reconnect assessment for learning and ensure that leadership and mentoring are on tap, every day, every week, every month, and every term and year throughout schooling. By doing so, the school not only creates better teachers and learners, but it also creates a system that allows people to be who they were meant to be: people. This is also the basis for the teams and problem solvers of the knowledge society.

The model created is set out below (Figure 12.2).

It is now possible to fill in the blanks.

1. Identify customers and specify value: For parent customers, value is having an opportunity to contribute and be involved in a meaningful way with their child's school experience. Parents do not want a school that is simply safe and free from bullying; they want a school where there is a named person(s) who knows their child well and one with whom they can talk and especially so at critical (learning) times. They want to be assured that their child is achieving and to help as necessary. Children need support from adults and older students, affirmation.

2. Identify and map the value stream: The value stream of support for learning involves putting in place the end-to-end operational process that delivers value to the customer in a high-quality way. All users have to understand how such interconnectivity works and be able to manage the information flow needed.

3. Create flow by eliminating waste: In building our systems thinking school, the school has to move from back-office deliverology to front-office interconnectivity. Any practices, policies, and procedures, which do not contribute to effective communication and to learning, require removal. This particularly includes linear management ways.

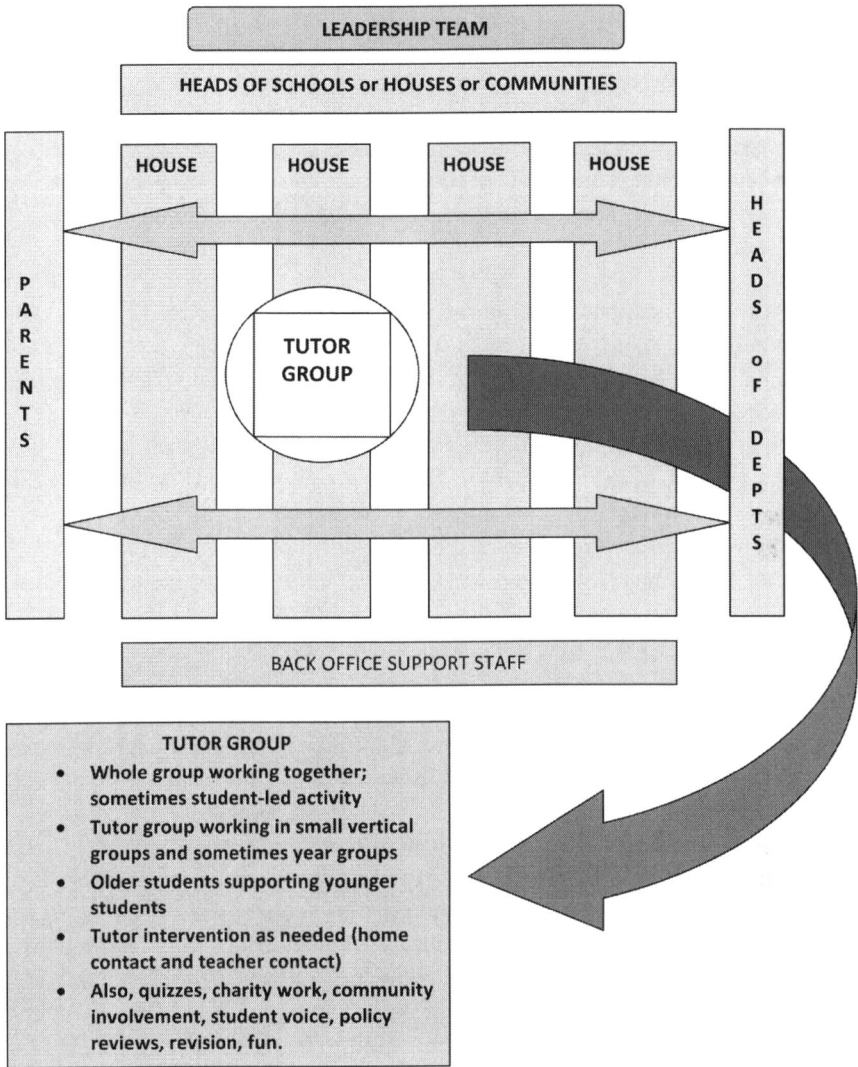

Figure 12.2.

4. Respond to customer pull: VT is a system that relies on adherence to tight organizational principles and values in the set-up stage (where most schools struggle and assume). Schools have to be adaptive and current. Parents and the community they represent are key to reconnecting with the wider knowledge society. By getting these learning and working relationships right, such adaptation should be far easier

as systemic change, probably based on individualized learning models, come to the fore.

5. Pursue perfection: The understanding of *flow and pull* enables the school to be adaptive and able to constantly improve its organizational operations around learning and communication, attention to system management. The key is to ensure that every child is supported on his or her learning journey as needed. In fact, the school can only function if every child is supported in a personal and professional way.

Strangely, we have every reason for optimism. Our amazing teachers continue to show astonishing capability in making a system that is well past its sell-by date appear to work at least in some areas. They often succeed despite the system, building and cherishing relationships. They have also shown remarkable resilience and altruism in being able to take so much criticism, most of which is undeserved. They remain heroic and wrongly maligned. Meanwhile, the price paid in well-being is high for all concerned, and the outcomes in performance, health, and opportunity for US students remains unacceptable.

One thing is absolutely clear. Any systems thinking school cannot have a solely horizontal basis on which to build learning relationships and support. It is regrettable having to repeat this so many times, but such wrong-headed thinking needs to be challenged. Leadership colleges and teacher training institutions cannot continue to endorse linear and split systems that do not work and then train teachers, managers, and leaders into believing that they do! Schools must have a vertical dimension, albeit for only twenty minutes each day, to enable all learning relationships to form, and to benefit from full communications interconnectivity.

This is the start of tidying up the system mess and rethinking content and learning. School principals who disagree should look again at Shukla's taxonomy (1994). The many principals and head teachers I do meet are those that ask for help from fellow travelers; as Nicholas Ind (2012) reminds us, leading "requires humility, self knowledge and constant customer dialogue." School leadership must be party to the business of growing a learning process and ensuring that everyone is connected to it, to more of itself. This is not some pious dream but is eminently doable.

The totality of the school's human resources has to be assembled to make this cultural change. In many ways this book has followed the path Margaret Wheatley (1999) mapped out in her ideas on principles for how life self-organizes and changes:

- A living system forms itself as it recognizes shared interests.
- For change to occur, there must be a change in meaning.
- Every living system is free to choose whether it will change or not.
- To create a healthier system, connect it to more of itself.

A change in meaning is important. Care is not what it seems; targets masquerade as aids to improvement; tests test abilities to pass tests rather than to engage in any learning substance; systemic change is not always what it claims to be, a school self-improvement system is not improvement, leadership training is not the right leadership training, children are left behind. I set out these and many other semantics in *Chaos, Culture and Third Millennium Schools* (Barnard, 2000) more than a decade ago. The schools I meet at least listen; many decide to change and so create something better, something that actually works. They can become places where words and actions have meaning and where values are not so easily assumed or discounted.

They wish to do exactly as Wheatley suggests: create a healthier school by connecting it to more of itself.

Chapter Thirteen

Assessment for Learning

> In organizations, real power and energy is generated through relationships.
> The patterns of relationships and the capacities to form them are more impor-
> tant than tasks, functions, roles, and positions.
> —Margaret Wheatley, 1999

Having created a system capable of handling a large increase in information flow, both in-house and between home and school in a quality way, it is a question of deciding the nature of the information needed to improve outcomes and enhance the quality of learning and teaching.

It has always been a great fascination to hear schools talk about *assessment for learning* (AfL). Seconds after sitting through a three-hour talk on this subject, I realized that I was unable to remember a thing including my own name! It was difficult to remember what the point actually was in relation to the systems in use. The speaker was used to horizontal systems, not vertical, and this created all sorts of organizational restrictions on this important area. Although summative assessment involved a judgment of learning achievement over time, the speaker was unable to fully explain the theory about how diagnostic or formative assessment might inform better teaching. If it did, it would not be unreasonable to see a rise in innovative teaching rather than a continuation of the same.

It may be that the reason for this is that in a linear system the assessment for learning or interconnectivity loop needed for summative and formative assessment fails to properly form. They tend to be treated as quite separate entities and then get somehow stuck in the classroom. We seem to have a situation whereby summative assessment is largely seen as the "parents' bit," which allows schools to use minimal levels and grades to describe fifteen thousand hours of schooling. Meanwhile formative assessment, for which so much is claimed, is not being used in the exciting ways pundits hope. It seems that without a coherent means of better summative assessment, there is no effective means of formative change. Part of the reason for this puzzle, this separation of assessment in the linear model seems to relate to the separation of the teacher and tutor role. This requires explanation.

In schools with VT, it is recognized that to improve and support learning requires a number of different things to happen congruently. In a vertical and more personalized system, everyone is a tutor by default and so all teachers and managers find themselves at the center of the communications and information network for a small group of students. The tutor (everyone) is the person gauging the student's performance overview; he is the junction box of the information system able to make an assessment of information from home, from his tutor group, and from monitoring formative assessments and reports. This is a rich combination of affective and summative information, information that has the potential to inform better teaching and learning practices but information that is largely inaccessible and unusable in linear systems.

The vertical system demands that information transcend data and should provide much better descriptors of the whole child as a learner by including strategies for personal improvement. Although tutors may receive this summatively, over time, they are in a position to monitor classroom progress and be in receipt of important information from home contact. In fact, the tutor (who is, invariably, also a teacher) has a clear picture of a tutee's performance: summative assessment is no longer hampered by time lag. This places the tutor in a unique position to advise on formative changes both in house and out.

Previous chapters show how every player in the linear model is undermined and prevented from doing his or her job well because of ineffective feedback loops. Teachers cannot communicate sufficiently, and so offer limited data out. Parents are largely isolated and hamstrung by the paucity of the summative data they receive; this renders them ineffective (poor parents) and causes delays to effective intervention leading to complaint demand (waste and flow issues). Subsequently homes offer little information, especially if relationships fail. Tutors are not effectively involved in any linear system no matter how much the school managers contort the organizational arrangement. This has been described throughout. It achieves stasis.

In the linear model, it is left for the parents to somehow do the summative job, but with almost no relevant data available to them. This is not easy given the jargon, the grades, and restricted language that schools increasingly use to presumably keep parents at bay! They receive limited information at the time it cannot be used! But in essence, AfL should be quite simple. That is, it started *simple* and then it hit the horizontal common cause variation problem and became problematic.

All schools realize that AfL is the important stuff and all have AfL policies and AfL coordinators, but in the systems that schools operate, all of this continues to be undermined by blockages that prevent the AfL cycle from completing successfully. We all know that AfL should inspire innovation and new teaching and learning techniques. The problem is not with teachers who are always keen to do better by the kids, but the school's understanding of how to best manage the communication and information network needed to make AfL work.

AFL AND BLACK BOXES

Paul Black and Dylan Wiliam (1998) continue to make exceptional contributions to our understanding of schools as organizations and to learning and teaching in particular. It is worth looking again at their influential work *Inside the Black Box*, which is packed with sound systems thinking.

The black box is the classroom and governments feed in endless demands, reforms, add-ons, and fixes to make the classroom and the teachers and the students who inhabit such places, work better. These include the mess of testing, examination systems, school changes, vocational diplomas now seen as dumbing down by some, performance league tables, equivalencies now being criticized and undone, moving averages and grades, tiering arrangements also viewed as suspicious, key stages now being reviewed, SATs, ongoing changes to inspection regimes, leadership training schemes, and so forth. To call the amalgam of these constructs confusing is an understatement, but they form the rickety, sticky-tape architecture of schooling.

Black and Wiliam (1998) rightly point out that "the sum of these doesn't add up to an effective policy because something is missing." For Black and Wiliam, all of these add-ons actually make the tasks of teachers more difficult and more complex. Of themselves, they are a good reason for being unable to use formative assessment creatively. What teachers actually need besides trust and less state interference, they say, is a reminder of the many different assessment strategies available to them, and to be offered the encouragement and support to use them. But the system problem of constant change and add-ons described does not melt away and remains a constant barrier to refining teaching and learning techniques (special cause). Peripheral changes and tinkering cannot address fundamentals.

Now, a decade on, and despite all of the AfL work and knowledge that exists, something should have shifted in terms of pedagogical outcomes and strategies—but it has not. Black and Wiliam (2001) proposed four ways for improving AfL, and they begin with one of the great statements about school systems, the kind of statement it is so easy to pass by.

Teachers will not take up attractive sounding ideas, albeit based on extensive research, if these are presented as general principles which leave entirely to them the task of translating them into everyday practice—their classroom lives are too busy and too fragile for this to be possible for all but an outstanding few.

The paradox is this. We cannot build a system on the outstanding few and neither can we make all teachers outstanding given the system we have. Our outstanding teachers are actually a systems problem! They are so amazing that they actually make it seem as though the broken system in which they operate can work, and this, paradoxically, is a major obstacle for those wanting qualitative systemic change. Otherwise, kids are pushed over the target finish line as best teachers can in the time teachers have according to the targets and tests set out. UK kids, incidentally, are the most tested in the world and this dulls most appetites for innovation.

In a world of tests, the classroom becomes test-dominant, blotting out the intrinsic nature of real learning. The problem is that any such target-driven approach is not learning in any real sense, but rather education with gaps and short cuts, and it shows in our national exasperation over outcomes and in the information we choose to share with parents and the kids who deserve so much more. One critic described US education as "Swiss cheese," education with holes! In simple terms, AfL involves gathering information about learning so that teachers and learners can decide where the student is, where he or she needs to go, and how best to get there.

From this point, everything gets hopelessly messy and the concept eventually gets buried alongside a zillion other failed strategies. The classroom should rightly be the focus for risk, new approaches and ideas, teamwork, and so forth but cannot function optimally without the interconnection to the powerful (when in place) tutor-parent-student trinity where much of the information needed is gathered and reformulated. Neither can it be fully operational if waste accumulates restricting flow.

The key to AfL and any subsequent improvement to teaching and learning methodology is actually a school-wide matter and as Black and Wiliam infer, it does not start within the classroom. They set out their scheme for the development of AfL under the heading Learning for Development, Dissemination, Reducing Obstacles and Further Research. Systems thinking is concerned with reducing obstacles (waste) and building a better learning process. Under the Obstacles section is this statement, which goes right to the heart of the school's learning and improvement challenge (Wiliam and Black 1998):

All teachers have to undertake some summative assessment, for example to report to parents, and to produce end-of-year reports as classes are due to move on to new teachers. However, the task of assessing pupils summatively for external purposes is clearly different from the task of assessing ongoing work to monitor and improve progress. Some argue that these two roles are so different that they should be kept apart. We do not see how this can be done, given that teachers must have some share in responsibility for the former and must take the leading responsibility for the latter. Indeed, from the information that teachers gather for formative purposes, they should, with selection and re-interpretation, be in a strong position to contribute to a fair summative report on each pupil.

Black and Wiliam are discussing breakages in critical learning and teaching loops. Although this is classic systems thinking at the checking and knowledge stage, it is the system redesign, the resolution that is missing, and without this, things get a lot worse for the parent, the teacher, and the learner. Besides, the kinds of reports that are sent home invite no information back. Such reports are simply lists of grades and targets with hardly a mention of AfL as an ongoing conversation between school, child, and caregivers. The school reduces summative assessment to minimal requirements, while formative assessment ticks over, perhaps measuring where a child is. Nothing much seems to change.

VT as an organizational culture provides the potential to get AfL back on track. Formative and summative assessments are two sides of the same learning and teaching coin and are integral to the school's information system and to handling customer demand and variation issues. They are in effect the main substance of interconnectivity, the ongoing deep learning conversation between teachers, students, and parents facilitated by tutors, most of whom are also teachers. Although teachers will try and ensure student success in whatever system they work, the linear model isolates teachers and departments from the rest of the organization and from customers.

This can fundamentally change the nature of how they perceive the value work they do and this means erring on the teaching side rather than the learning. In turn, this can distort assessment. It is a kind of catch-22. Teachers are concerned about coverage and test results and these do not always bode well for experimentation and engagement as the dropout surveys suggest. Reports for summative assessment tend to be numbers and grades used to measure progress in time. Sadly, parents are left to make what sense of these they can, but in the absence of an infill of relevant communication, support, and intervention such assessments can often turn out to be full of unpleasant surprises. It is hardly customer care.

Sometimes, schools have tried to resolve this formative and summative matter by designating school managers as leaders of learning, learning managers, or even leadership and assessment managers. None really works despite the effort such high-quality people put in. Fortunately, the cultural organization of VT provides a simple means of resolving the AfL dichotomy.

THE VERTICAL TUTORING SYSTEMS THINKING SOLUTION

The key is to change mind-sets. Although there is nothing wrong with the many strategies schools promote to inspire greater engagement in learning and promote more effective teaching (including ideas like three-part lessons, lesson observation and what Hargreaves [2006] calls *co-construction*) these all pertain to the linear model and are insufficient to do the job required. The remedy has to involve making both summative and formative assessment work as intended, and that means as a whole-school or whole-system improvement strategy, one that everyone owns.

This means changing other mind-sets. Student engagement must not be seen solely as the challenge to be met by entertaining teachers. Students have to be on board by extending co-construction so that it involves parents and the tutors. VT sets out the interconnectivy needed for information to flow and affirmation to work; it improves learning relationships. The missing bit is assessment information. What VT demands as a whole system is high-quality information to loop throughout the school in a way that tutors, student mentors, parents, and learners can make best use of. Grades and levels (numbers) are insufficient; the learning conversation must involve strategies for improvement and more—critical information each player and combination of players can use to make progress.

VT, via the tutors, invites the teacher back into the whole school to share with parents the child's learning journey, what the child needs to make progress. Summative assessment belongs to everyone but especially the tutor, the child, and the parent who work to support formative classroom assessment by intervening and contributing to overall strategies for improvement. In effect a learning climate is created.

When children feel more supported and confident because of the learning relationships developed in tutor time, they take this to the classroom. When student mentors lead and develop greater self-esteem and self-respect, they also take this to the classroom. When teachers act as tutors, as all must do in a VT system, they are not only seen by students differently and more respectfully, but they realize the importance of summative information in their tutorial function and the link with formative change when they go to the classroom. They also realize just how much support from parents there is. When attitudes change, AfL makes so much more organizational sense; it becomes part of the culture rather than a classroom add-on.

Realistically, tutors are summative assessors but not just from semester to semester but weekly and even daily. It is a task they share with parents, enabling better conversations with learners and more rapid interventions. Once a community is involved in the language of learning, risk-taking and innovative ideas reflect such an organizational mind-set. What drives such an organization is a hunger for change and doing things better rather than resistance and stasis. It is not assessment that drives the school but the school and the customer that drive assessment.

What the trinity of parent, child, and tutor does is to constantly engage in rich summative conversations and especially so at critical times; these inform the learning process with regard to formative changes to learning need and support. Put simply, when all players operate and accept responsibility for learning as a complete, double-loop learning operation, they feel connected not only to more of themselves but also to a greater purpose.

It is part of what Jonathan Haidt (2006) identified in *The Happiness Hypothesis* as the key to being happy and leading a virtuous and meaningful life.

> Just as plants need sun, water and good soil to thrive, people need love, work and a connection to something larger. It is worth striving to get the right relationship between yourself and others, between yourself and your work, and between yourself and something larger than yourself. If you get these relationships right a sense of purpose and well-being will emerge.

It is this (inter)connectivity that creates the double loops and multi-feedback learning processes built on learning relationships. It is this that should inspire the release of creativity as the main feature and raison d'être of all organizations, which, like schools, exist to release the latent potential of those who walk their corridors.

And what of those who hanker after full systemic change? Such changes get the schools back in systems thinking mode, in a condition of health that enables discussion and planning to take place. The school can discharge itself from the acute-pain ward of the reform hospital and get back to work more independently minded, stronger, and more able to talk about the knowledge society, the commons, and what is needed to be part of Gaia (Lovelock, 1979).

Schools are there to grow these relationships, to connect people to more of themselves, and enable young people to learn what is important, of value, and how to do battle with paradoxes and with those who keep dismantling things to see how they work and are unable to put them back together.

LEARNING CONVERSATIONS AND CRITICAL TIMES

In lean organizations this is where pull theory really starts to work as a new customer focus and revived customer relationship grows. For families and for schools, besides ongoing monitoring and assessment there are critical learning times in a child's schooling when everyone, the main caregivers, the student, and the tutor, needs to pool information and decide strategies for improvement rather than targets for achievement alone. At such key times, they need to talk, gather and share information, be able to intervene, pull down the necessary resources needed, and revise their support tactics to proceed and secure positive outcomes and greater achievement.

Identifying these critical times dictates AfL in part, and must be among the first items on the school's academic calendar. At these times, the key home, school, and child learning conversations or *academic tutorials* take place. The secondary schools and middle schools will identify the first critical time around six weeks after the new entrants join the school. This is a key settling-in time when the school, parents, and child should review progress and make sure everything is on track and remains that way.

It is a time when new students have got to know the school, its routines, and its personnel. It is also a time when young people can elect to drop out of learning for a long period unnoticed by the school and by parents. Another obvious critical learning and assessment time is at the end of the first year and another is the follow-up to tests and the lead-in to examinations. Such critical times need to be identified because these determine when all players need to talk, take stock, agree about strategies for improvement, and plan any ongoing monitoring and support needed. Such learning conversations or academic tutorials are tutor led and take about forty minutes.

What is noticeable in the horizontal system is that critical times for assessment and reports are largely ignored in favor of convenient times, and deep information (summative and formative combined) is swapped for lists of grades, levels, and targets that do not translate easily into improved teaching and learning and the enabling job that students, parents, and tutors need to do. Full academic tutorials do not exist in any substantive form.

ACADEMIC TUTORIALS OR DEEP LEARNING CONVERSATIONS

The nature of parents' evenings in horizontal systems is fraught with time challenges and assessment difficulties. Rich and useful conversations and actions rarely materialize. The settling-in meeting in horizontal schools is usually optional, an *opportunity* for parents rather than a *requirement*; the data available is minimalistic and generalist to the point of being close to unusable: usually attendance and possibly a little on behavior and attitude thrown in.

What should be an important and vital occasion for discussing formative and summative matters is close to customer abuse (not forgetting that everyone is a customer). Not only are critical information loops weakened, they are too often intentionally sold to parents as *opportunities*, something not really important or necessary, a system add-on. It seems that schools are now loaded with the mess of untaken opportunities as a replacement for the partnered management of learning.

VT takes a different line. It begins by engaging with parents to identify all critical learning times in the lives of children; a time when parents, school, and the child need to talk, review what teachers are saying, and agree on strategies for support and improvement (not setting targets as such but certainly trying to make sense of them). To handle this demand, manage variation and build value in, the reporting and assessment system of the school is re-engineered and aligned to these critical times where they can be of most use.

It is imperative that the systems thinking school offers a full written report at all critical times, not just data sheets. This allows parents, tutors, and child the chance to reflect, intervene, and plan and agree to strategies for improvement. Instead of having to meet 25-plus students and parents in an evening and rely on the fact that not everyone will turn up, the lead tutor and co-tutor have only to meet a maximum of four families over a one-week period and this changes everything.

This enables customer care and quality service combine to as follows.

1. VT establishes a personalized learning partnership by providing parents with an essential liaison link to the school via their child's tutor as the learning and information conduit.
2. Because of VT, co-construction is now active and parental and child input is essential in ascertaining agreed-upon strategies for further progress, effectively establishing the tutor and parent partnership role as the key to successful formative and summative assessment for learning.
3. Meetings with parents are likely to be forty minutes long not five minutes, relaxed, and valued, where all parties can contribute. These are underpinned by a full written report, not just levels and grades. Such an academic tutorial shares critical report information at a critical learning time and here are spread over the year as needed.
4. Parents are offered any after-school slot they like to meet with tutors within the framework of a week outside of the teaching day, not a single slot on an inconvenient night.
5. The relationship between parent, tutor, and child is another powerful unit of in-group loyalty able to intervene when the aspiration gene is endangered and acts as a stable and permanent back-up. Parents and tutors support each other and allow the customer care constructs of intimacy and trust to form.
6. Once everybody in the system understands their role and how everything is connected to everything else, innovation is possible and the school is limited only by its corporate ability to be creative.
7. All children are engaged in the learning process through their leadership and mentoring input, enabling strong mixed-age loyalty groups to

form as counters to any unwanted social pressures and negativity often associated with peer groups.

8. The academic tutorial produces agreed-upon strategies for improvement that enjoy daily support and intervention from the tutor.

Sadly, after a decade of assessment for learning, it seems we have reduced our kids to a set of meaningless grades and levels, incomprehensible to most families, which are sent home three times a year with targets attached. In every one of the hundreds of horizontal schools I have been to and trained, it was possible for every single child to go through school without touching the sides, without ever having a proper conversation and opportunity to reflect on learning with parents present and with someone from the school who knew the child well.

VT returns the school to a full learning conversation between child, school, and parent, a full information exchange based on simple customer care principles moving from a back-office bureaucracy to a high-quality front office values system. It really is that simple.

Chapter Fourteen

Concluding Remarks

Inspiration, hunger: these are the qualities that drive good schools. The best we educationists can do is create the most likely conditions for them to flourish, and then get out of the way.

—Ted Sizer, 1984

The two systems can be set out as follows in this much abbreviated list.

Adding a small vertical dimension to the way a school operates transforms it into a learning organization. It becomes self-managing and emergent. There are other differences hinted at in Table 14.1 that are just as important and they run deep. A systems thinking school is sure of its path and more independently minded. This means it can make better decisions and take its community with it, and this gives it spiritual strength, coherence, purpose, and relevance. It is more purely values-driven. This is what Peter Senge and colleagues set out in part in *Schools that Learn* (2000). Such schools are not afraid to speak the language of systemic purpose and know what is needed to achieve this. Fred Kofman and Peter Senge (2001) put it as follows:

Deep learning, then, is not a matter of figuring out the truth. Deep learning is the embodiment of new capabilities for effective action. Embodiment is a developmental process that occurs over time, in a continuous cycle of theoretical action and practical conceptualization. The impatient quest for improvement all too often results in superficial changes that leave deeper patterns untouched. Herein lays the core leadership paradox: Action is critical, but the action we need can spring only from a reflective stance.

Horizontal (Year/Grade)	Systems Thinking (Vertical)
Low Mentoring Opportunities	Mentoring Opportunities for All
Lower-Order Tutor Skills: Impersonal	High-Order Tutor Skills: Individualized
Variable Student /Tutor Attention	Focused Attention by Need
Behavior Dominated	Collaboration/Learning Dominated
High Stress and High Control	Low Stress and Shared Control: Collaborative
Leadership Opportunities for the Few	Leadership Opportunities for All
Year Ethos Difficulties	House Ethos Opportunities + Year Ethos
Tutor Isolated by Year	Tutor Integrated by House and Learning Process
Poor Flow: Low Level information	Improved Information and Flow
No Effective Academic Tutorial	Deep Learning Conversations at Critical Times
Weak Parental Partnership/Engagement	Strong Parental Engagement in Learning Process
Tutors as Low Status Staff	Tutors as High Status Front-Line Staff
Big Tutor Groups: Few Tutors	Small Tutor Groups: Everyone a Tutor
Complicated Processes/Policies	Clarity of Process: Interconnectivity Throughout
High Behavior Management (extrinsic)	Higher Intrinsic Behavior / Learning / Motivation
High Potential for Bullying & Suspensions & Dropouts	Low Bullying / Fewer Suspensions / Lower Gang Influence/less dropouts
Weak Student Voice System	Strong Student Voice System
Weak Assessment for Learning	Strong Assessment for Learning: Interconnected
Variable Emotional Intelligence	Higher Emotional Intelligence
Incomplete Assessment for Learning	Formative and Summative Assessment Integrated
Variable in Spiritual Intelligence	High EQ, and SQ
Low in System Innovation	High Innovation and Ecological Adaptation
Low in Co-construction/Personalization	High in Co-construction/Personalization
Communications Loop Incomplete	Communications/ Learning Loops Complete
Limited Outcomes (Pass Rates) by Test	Unlimited Outcomes by Capability and Potential
High Common Cause Variation	Low Common Cause Variation

Figure 14.1.

SCHOOLS AS COMPLEX ORGANIZATIONS

David Sherwood (2002) advised that success as an organization requires a willingness to tackle complexity head-on and to use systems thinking to *describe, examine, and explore.* We need to dwell on the nature of schools one last time to dissolve a final paradox—the challenge of complexity.

Schools suffer heavy bureaucracy; are riddled with tricky procedures, practices, and protocols; and as a result many describe them as complex organizations. They are so complex, it seems, that they defy analysis. The truth and the paradox is that most of this complexity is actually fake—waste accumulation that arises because the linear model is actually far too simple. It assumes value and quality when in reality it separates itself in space and time from both. What has happened in schools is that for a long time they have remained unerringly simple in a world that has grown unerringly complex. The linear underpinning has made them unable to adapt to customer demand.

The critical flow of information has been all but blocked and interconnectivity denied.

There has been no means of adaption, no evolution, just an ongoing and wicked mess; single-loop *tinkering to utopia*; distortions thrown-up from the blueprint of the past. Ours is a failure to offer schools an outside view, a way out, and so we blame them instead for our own inadequacies just as Robert Trivers (2011) said we would.

Schools have insufficient means of communication, reduced information to a set of grades, disconnected teachers from the totality of the learning operation, ignored parents and customer care, and have been unable to innovate and evolve. All of the lesser matters about kids and well-being and parents are dumped on the linear tutor, also isolated within the system. When the tutor goes under, he or she is unable to be the person that the students and parents and school need him or her to be. Only in places of high compliance to such nonsense can such a system survive.

Systems thinking acts to remove the waste and reopen the channels of communication and so rebuild the interconnectivity between people, what connects them as opposed to what separates them. It serves to reinstate purpose and the deeper spiritual meaning of the value work that all schools seek to do. In effect, it replaces waste complexity with the sophisticated communications it needs and allows it to double-loop flow, feeding off the ideas produced and the creativity released.

It does this by leveraging system change at the level of meaning, inviting a new management vocabulary to form. It is systems thinking that signals the death of one paradigm and the beginning of another. All that VT does is to allow schools to be adaptive, to manage the chaotic interim, and face the future as confident participants. VT also adds the dimension and the power needed to rebuild the learning pathways and light them in a way that supports learners and their teachers.

W. Edwards Deming (2000) believed that the first step to transformation is the individual. Such understanding requires what he called "profound knowledge":

- Appreciation for a system
- Knowledge about variation
- Theory of knowledge
- Psychology

These four points are precisely what is missing from school leadership and management programs. Even today, they provide a framework for change and innovation. These are big matters and we need to dwell on them. Schools have to somehow be so much more than they are, and that means management change.

Sometimes, when ideas like the horizontal system have been with us for generations, we simply fail to notice its limitations; it becomes part of the landscape. Teachers genuinely try and make such a system work for the kids but the odds are stacked against them. We keep returning and tinkering and too often the familiarity we have can breed the contempt we show despite the astonishing efforts schools make. But the fact is we prepare our children for something other than the *real* world. Alfie Kohn (1999), talking about the United States, said:

> We are a nation that prefers acting to thinking, and practice to theory, we are suspicious of intellectuals, worshipful of technology, and fixated on the bottom line. We define ourselves by numbers—take home pay and cholesterol counts, percentiles (how much does your baby weigh?) and standardized test scores (how much does your child know?).

Three years ago, an Oxford University philosophy professor, Tony Ord, decided to give half of his sixty-thousand-dollar salary to charity every year. A few have now followed this example. He said he did not need that much money to lead a good life. Somehow, in the United States, there has to be a return to values rather than the obscenities of inequality that exist. Only if our kids learn values and understand what it is to care through the experiences school offers, can we hope for a better society.

Deming suggested that when an individual understands the profound knowledge, he or she is transformed and will see new meaning to life. He or she will

- set an example.
- be a good listener, but will not compromise.
- continually teach other people.
- help people to pull away from their current practice and beliefs and move into the new philosophy without a feeling of guilt about the past.

The first three describe the role of the vertical tutor or mentor and the fourth tells systems thinkers what they must do. The more we *look* as Robert Fulghum advised, the more it is possible to see schools as victims of essentially extrinsic motivators butting up against the intuition of intrinsically driven people. It creates an illusory Schoolworld that never has to deal with any real issues.

So what has all of this to do with schools, purpose, systems thinking, and change?

It was seven years after her death that Meadow's last book, *Thinking in Systems* (2009), was published. Like so many systems thinkers, she reflected on the kind of quantitative scientific thinking that had created so much success and the qualitative thinking needed to secure our future. Meadows believed that systems "self-organize. . . . The most marvellous characteristic of some complex systems is their ability to learn, diversify, complexify, evolve."

She believed that this process of self-organization that had been so successful, that had got us where we are, seems to be hesitating. Our world has become one of short-term gains, the myth of the American dream, happiness from a ten-point plan, shrinks on speed dial, consumerism, and ecological apathy: single-loop capitalism rather than double-loop. Surely, this wicked stuff that our children face needs our schools and our teachers to sort it all out, but this can only be done by creating schools driven by values and partnered by families and nested in secure communities.

VERTICAL TUTORING

And this is the challenge. Can we produce learning organizations of kids that will ultimately want less and can give more? Kids able to work better than we did; kids able to stand back and understand systems thinking and interconnections; kids able to walk the talk of values, kids that care? I am still hopeful having worked with thousands of them and with their teachers who never give up on this. Most still dream real American Dreams and we are fortunate that they do.

Systems thinking must get the school as a community to a point where it can actively think and practice meaning and purpose—where it can innovate, ask questions, and make its own intuitive judgments. Some call this learning. Systems thinking should be the start of the self-organization and emergence stage when schools reactivate learning as a whole school and community process to discover what is truly important. Systems thinking is limited. Although it can point out the double loops needed for more spiritual, learning organizations to form, the journey still has to be made.

This book is an attempt to get us to that point in a journey where the ecological reasons for change, the gaps between schools and society, are too compelling to ignore. I respect that schools cannot change much of their context and little of their content at the moment, but these barriers will fall when the school feels itself getting stronger, more able to make learning and teaching more personally and operationally effective—more able to flow, pull and lean, and more able to lead a learning conversation rather than lag behind.

VT adheres to no ideology. It is simple and complex at the same time and enables conversations about learning to take place in safe and exciting ways that respect participants. It is a system that can replace the prevailing linear culture bit by bit but with the urgency needed. It is a double-loop learning system driven by values and strong management principles, not logistics. It can do the math and handle numbers individually.

The purpose here is to show how to harness the incredible resilience and strength latent in self-organizing schools at zero cost. The nested vertical system is simple. A school is an adult, a child, an older kid, and a world of interconnected information. The learning process is an interconnectivity of people engaging in learning in ways that are fun and safe and risky all at the same time. It is how the child, the adults, and the school all learn and reflect together, how everyone uses and reveals their talents to make the marginal gains and then the bigger wins. This is what VT works to enable.

Nothing is off the tutor and child's learning agenda. Summative and formative matters combine. The school reconnects the parts made disparate by industrial thinking by highlighting the natural interconnectivity of good people engaged in a conversation with our kids about learning; it is part of a learning process and *community of commitment* that is fun and has a universal feel. It is a journey back from the extrinsic to the intrinsic where, in Kohn's words, we cannot be so easily *Punished by Rewards* (1999).

Such schools arrive at a crossroads where they can look back at the road traveled and the one ahead. The road traveled is littered with the debris of failed initiatives, reforms that shone and died, broken learning relationships, and lives that could have been better. The way ahead is blocked by unresolved paradoxes and lit by signposts you can no longer trust, where the geography is uncertain. That does not matter when the school is one that intuitively sticks together rather than one that is stuck together. It is all about management and holding hands.

SYSTEM THINKING LAWS

Bertalanffy said there were system laws waiting to be discovered. We should not expect those laws to be accurately described and quantified, but might discover some of them through strange pathways perhaps like Robert Pirsig's metaphysical search, his own *Inquiry into Values* (2006). If systems thinking does anything, it is to make practical our methods and processes for acting on what is right. Daniel Goleman (1995) introduced us to emotional intelligence (EQ), a journey from IQ to EQ.

Learning relationships are fundamentally built on the basis of EQ, which, for me, should precede SEL programs and reduce their need. The real organizational and learning journey is from EQ to spiritual intelligence (SQ). It is Danar Zohar and Ian Marshall (2001) who offered us SQ to access our deeper meanings and purposes especially in the context of organizations and systems. The systems thinking journey for schools is from IQ to EQ to SQ and is adapted here.

SQ applies not only to people but also to organizations like schools where the underlying purpose is to garner and create the spiritual capital needed for a more sustainable, thoughtful, and better world. Howard Gardner (1983) proposed recognition of a number of intelligences to better enable this. He too was concerned that children should understand the world and be able to make it a better place. Teachers like this idea because it ties in with their experience that children have different talents and styles that deserve to be recognized and valued.

Systems thinking, of course, looks slightly aslant at such analyses and seeks to join them all up again to realize their interconnectivity.

Among Zohar and Marshall's (2001) principles of transformation are the following (slightly adapted here). Schools should consider these as they journey to spiritual and organizational intelligence.

- Be self-aware—live with space and silence.
- Be holistic—see the big picture.
- Have a vision—be led by your values.
- Take risks and innovate—learn from failure.
- Stand out against the crowd—be a good Samaritan.
- Be open to diversity—reframe and stand back.
- Advance to the edge—be a little uncomfortable.

As Zohar and Marshall suggest, such processes encourage us to enter the domains of chaos and quantum mechanics whereby systems constantly overlap and change leading to the emergence of something more adaptive, current, and new. All we need do is to make sure that *new* is better. Bertalanffy's laws are not easy to pin down because they are metaphysical in essence. Meadows saw it this way: the parenthetical comments are my weak interpretations for schools. Think of schools as mixed-age collaborations.

1. Get the beat of the system. (Feel the school as a living entity; stand way back and see.)
2. Expose your mental models to the light of day. (Return to knowledge; spot any assumptions.)

Capital	Intelligence	Purpose	System
Material	IQ: Rational	I think	Teacher/learner extrinsic loop: Single-loop: linear
Social	EQ: Emotional	I feel	Holistic learning relationships: Double-loop: vertical
Spiritual	SQ: Spiritual	I am	Holistic + intrinsic learning: double and open feedback loops (VT)

Figure 14.2.

3. Honor, respect, and distribute information. (Build learning relationships and interconnectivity.)
4. Use language with care and enrich it with systems concepts. (Adopt management vocabularies.)
5. Pay attention to what is important not just what is quantifiable. (Be led by values.)
6. Make feedback policies for feedback systems. (Design the double loops and manage them.)
7. Go for the good of the whole. (See the big picture and aspire to greater well-being and good.)
8. Listen to the wisdom of the system. (Be aware of SQ; listen at the periphery.)
9. Locate responsibility within the system. (See the school as a complete learning process for all.)
10. Stay humble, stay a learner. (Everyone is a teacher, everyone is a learner: ask when you get stuck.)
11. Celebrate complexity. (Welcome diversity and make it work for you. Embrace challenge.)
12. Expand time horizons. (Reorganize time: enable conversations, support, reflection, and planning.)
13. Defy the disciplines. (Approach learning as an exercise in discovery; start wicked journeys.)
14. Expand the boundary of caring. (Redefine care: move beyond the pastoral to the holistic.)
15. Do not erode the goal of goodness. (Listen and look: follow pathways that have real purpose.)

The reason I like VT is simple: it brings people together and values them. It enables them to aspire and ensures that work works. It produces better outcomes, builds quality in, and is life-affirming and bio-ecologically sound. It is built on systems thinking principles and so has a systems thinking capability that enables schools to reconnect to more of themselves, returning them to their value work, for those schools willing to unlearn and relearn. It also follows Deming's view of wisdom.

If we are unable to discern good practice from within our organizations, we need to look elsewhere. We do not have to look far; the living metaphor occupied much time in the United Kingdom during the summer of 2012.

LEARNING FROM THE 2012 PARALYMPICS

Much of the success of the London Olympics was owed to the games makers. These were the tens of thousands of people from all walks of life, young and old, who volunteered to help out, to guide, to give directions, to assure, to support, and to enable. The organizers of the games simply provided a purpose that enabled the games makers to be themselves, to be who we needed them to be. Once they knew the freedom of the system and its purpose, the rest was just fun.

But there was so much more. The paralympics sought to create a fair playing field, to reveal all the talents that were there, to celebrate and recognize variation, embrace complexity, and understand human potential in all its forms; and therein was the spiritual purpose. One athlete from the United Kingdom's sitting volleyball team was quoted by Sebastian Coe in his closing speech at the 2012 Paralympic Games in London. She said what the games had meant to her: *It is as if the cloud of limitation has been lifted.* Many schools aspire to do this for their teachers and students; their leaders are humble enough to seek advice and knowledge rather than a life of hand-me-down assumptions and ignorance.

Everyone participated in the learning journey made possible by the games makers, so much so that many talk of a spiritual change throughout the United Kingdom and beyond—a paradigm shift. There is a sense in the United Kingdom, perhaps short-lived, that priorities have shifted, well-being improved, and a more reflective world enabled—a world put into a sharper more caring perspective—an increase in goodness.

And when we left, the games makers were there to say good bye, to help us find our way home one last time—their leadership, support, and mentoring reliably present. We had all learned from the experience much more about values and what it is to see more clearly how to lead a good life, a helpful life where you put in so much more than you take out. Many learned during that two weeks more than they ever thought possible.

These are deeply interconnected and spiritual matters and are the real purpose of schools enabled by VT and systems thinking. Schools are there to produce good people, to recognize talent, and to make sure that there are no limitations. Yet, in our schools today, it is still possible for young people to go through them without ever being known in any deep sense, in places where speaking, the essence of what it is to be human, is banned and where young people are so narrowly measured and assessed. They can pass right through like shadows, barely touching the sides, most without anyone noticing they were there. This could never happen in a trained VT school, ever!

Despite this, our schools churn out amazing people, poets, singers, artists, thinkers, builders, scientists, and more. Kids survive the system and some even thrive.

Many schools have allowed me to share their company on their journey albeit for a short while. Without exception, they are populated by people who, rightly or wrongly, are amazing in their optimism and altruism; most still love their work and students and parents appreciate their efforts. Schools are not of their own creation; we all have a hand in their design. They contain people of seemingly limitless talent, patience, and potential, and we need to cherish them. If ever you want to feel hope and happiness, walk into a school. The spirit of the place, what gardeners call the *genius loci*, still lingers in most.

Some schools are evolving: they are experimenting with mixed-age teaching with astonishing results and redefining what it is to care and learn. VT supplies the platform of support for such adventures. These mavericks do not have to innovate, to risk more failure, but they do. They keep trying to make things better despite the daft things many ask them to do. Some are beginning to trust their instincts and are more able to see intelligence as a multifaceted pathway where depth and breadth combine, and where education is a spiritual journey and school a place that cherishes.

We need our schools to readopt the goal of goodness and to grow the self-awareness in our children, which appreciates that their small system is an important part of a bigger system, each dependent on the other. Such values sometimes shine through when it is easier to comply. They simply do not stop trying despite the crazy folk who ask them to do crazy things. There is little in the way of advice that systems thinking can offer except perhaps this: stand well back, listen, look, and look again.

References and Resources

Ackoff, R. L. 1970. *A concept of corporate planning*. New York: John Wiley & Sons.

Ackoff, R. L. 1974. *Redesigning the future: A systems approach to societal problems*. New York: John Wiley & Sons.

Ackoff, R. L. 1979. The future of operational research is past. *Journal of Operational Research Society*, 30(2):93–104.

Ackoff, R. L. 1999. On passing through 80. *Systemic Practice and Action Research*, 12(4): 425–430.

Ackoff, R. L. 2004. Transforming the systems movement. Speech at the 3rd National Conference on Systems Thinking, Philadelphia, PA, May 2004.

Ackoff, R. L., and D. Greenburg. 2008. *Turning learning right side up: Putting education back on track*. Upper Saddle River, NJ: Pearson Education, Inc.

Argyris, C., and D. Schön. 1974. *Theory in practice: Increasing professional effectiveness*. San Francisco: Jossey-Bass.

Argyris, C., and D. Schön. 1978. *Organizational learning: A theory of action perspective*. Reading, MA: Addison Wesley.

Banathy, B. H. 1992. *A systems view of education: Concepts and principles for effective practice*. Englewood Cliffs, NJ: Educational Technology Publications.

Bandura, A. 1977. *Social learning theory*. Englewood Cliffs, NJ: Prentice Hall.

Barnard, P. A. 2000. *Chaos, culture and third millennium schools*. Guildford, UK: Apocalypse Press.

Barnard, P. A. 2010. *Vertical tutoring: Notes on school management, learning relationships and school improvement*. Surrey: Grosvenor House Publishing.

Bar-Yam, Y. 2004. *Making things work: Solving complex problems in a complex world*. Cambridge, MA: Complex Systems Institute and Knowledge Press.

Belbin, R. M. 1996. *The coming shape of organisation*. Oxford: Butterworth Heinemann.

Bertalanffy, L. von. 1968. *General systems theory: Foundations, development, applications*. New York: George Braziller, Inc.

Bhasin, S., and P. Burcher. 2004. Lean viewed as philosophy. *Journal of Manufacturing Technology Management*, 17(1):56–72.

Black, P., and Wiliam, D. 1998. Assessment and classroom learning. *Assessment in Education: Principles, Policy, & Practice* 5(1), March 1998.

Black, P., and D. Wiliam. 1998. Inside the black box: Raising standards through classroom assessment. *Phi Delta Kappan*, 80(2):139–148.

Black, P., and D. Wiliam. 2001. *Inside the black box: Raising standards through classroom assessment. Short final draft*. London: British Educational Research Association.

Borman, G. D., and N. M. Dowling. 2006. Longitudinal achievement effects of multi-year summer school: Evidence from the Teach Baltimore randomized field trial. *Educational Evaluation and Policy Analysis,* 28(1): 25–48.

Bowen, M. 1978. *Family therapy in clinical practice.* Northvale, NJ: Jason Aronson Inc.

Bowlby, J. 1969. *Attachment and loss.* Volume 1. London: Hogarth Press.

Bridgeland, J. M., J. J. Dilulio Jr., and K. B. Morison. 2006. *The silent epidemic: Perspectives of high school dropouts.* Washington, DC: Civic Enterprises.

Bronfenbrenner, U. 1977. Toward an experimental ecology of human development. *American Psychologist,* 32(7):513–531.

Bronfenbrenner, U. 1979. *The ecology of human development.* Cambridge, MA: Harvard University Press.

Bronfenbrenner, U. 1990. Discovering what families do. In D. Blankenhorn, S. Bayme, and J. B. Elshtain (eds.), *Rebuilding the Nest* (pp. 27–38). Milwaukee: Family Service America.

Camillus, J. C. 2008. Strategy as a wicked problem. *Harvard Business Review,* 86(5):98–106.

Cappannelli, G., and S. Cappannelli. 2004. *Authenticity: Simple strategies for greater meaning and purpose at work and home.* Cincinnati: Emmis Books.

Carnie, F. 2004. *Pathways to child friendly schools: A guide for parents.* Bristol: Human Scale Education.

Chase, R. B. 1978. *Where does the customer fit in a service sector organization? Harvard Business Review,* 56(6):137–142.

Chase, R. B. 2010. Revisiting 'Where does the customer fit in a service operation?' Background and future development of contact theory. In P. P. Maglio, C. A. Kieliszewski, J. C. Spohrer (eds.), *Handbook of Service Science,* pp. 11–18. New York: Springer.

Coleman, J. S. 1966. *Equality of educational opportunity (COLEMAN) study (EEOS).* Ann Arbor, MI: Inter-university Consortium for Political and Social Research. doi:10.3886/ICPSR06389.v3.

Cox, M., and B. Paley. 1997. Families as systems. *Annual Review of Psychology:* 48(1): 243–267. doi: 10.1146/annurev.psych.48.1.243.

Cuban, L. 2004. *The blackboard and the bottom line: Why schools can't be businesses.* Boston: Harvard University Press.

Deming, W. E. 1982-1986. *Out of the crisis.* Cambridge, MA: MIT Press.

Deming, W. E. 2993. *The New Economics for Industry, Government, Education* (2nd edition). Cambridge: MIT Press.

Deming, W. E. 1994. *The new economics for industry, government, education,* 2nd ed. Cambridge: Massachusetts Institute of Technology, Center for Advanced Educational Services.

Dooley, J. 1995. Cultural aspects of systemic change management. In Proceedings: ASQC Quality Conference QC95. Santa Clara, CA. http://www.well.com/user/dooley/culture.pdf. Accessed May 7, 2013.

Drucker, P. 1969. The age of *discontinuity–Guidelines to our changing society.* New York: Harper & Row.

Drucker, P. 2008. *The five most important questions you will ever ask about your organization.* San Francisco: Jossey-Bass.

Druckerman, P. 2012. *Bringing up bébé: One American Mother Discovers the Wisdom of French Parenting.* London: Doubleday.

Dubois, D. L., and H. A. Neville. 1997. Youth mentoring: Investigation of relationship characteristics and perceived benefits. *Journal of Community Psychology,* 25(3):227–234.

Dubois, D. L., B. E. Holloway, J. C. Valentine, and H. Cooper. 2002. Effectiveness of mentoring programmes for youth: A meta-analytic review. *American Journal of Community Psychology,* 30(2):157–197.

Duffy, F. M. 2007a. Dream! Create! Sustain!: Mastering the art and science of transforming school systems. *The F. M. Duffy Reports,* 12(2). The FM Duffy Group. http://www.thefmduffygroup.com/publications/reports/Vol12_No2_DreamCreateSustain.pdf. Accessed May 7, 2013.

Duffy, F. M. 2007b. Strapping wings on a caterpillar and calling it a butterfly: When systemic change is not systemic. *The F. M. Duffy Reports,* 12(3). The FM Duffy Group. http://

www.thefmduffygroup.com/publications/reports/ Vol12_No3_WhenSystemicChangeIsNotSystemic.pdf. Accessed May 7, 2013.

Duffy, F. M. 2008. The need for whole district transformation. www.futureminds.us/document/ needfordistrictleveltransformation.pdf. Accessed May 7, 2013.

Duffy, F. M. 2010. *Dream! Create! Sustain!: Mastering the art and science of transforming school systems.* Lanham, MD: Rowman and Littlefield Education.

Duffy, R. M. 2007. Educating change leaders about how to navigate systemic transformational change in school districts. *The F. M. Duffy Group.* Posted online May 31, 2007.

Duffy, F. M., and C. M. Reigeluth. 2008. The school system transformation (SST) protocol. *Educational Technology* 48(4):41–49.

Eckel, P., B. Hill, and M. Green. 1998. *On change: En-route to transformation.* Washington, DC: American Council on Education.

Edwards, A., and C. D'arcy. 2004. Relational agency and disposition in sociocultural accounts of learning to teach. *Educational Review.* 56(2):147–155.

Ehly, S. W., and S. C. Larsen. 1980. *Peer tutoring for individualized instruction.* Boston: Allyn and Bacon.

Emiliani, B. February 2008a. The equally important 'respect for people principle.' *Superfactory.com* newsletter. http://www.superfactory.com/articles/featured/2008/0802-emiliani-respect-people.html. Accessed May 7, 2013.

Emiliani, B. 2008b. *Practical lean leadership: A strategic leadership guide for executives.* Kensington, CT: The CLBM, LLC.

Epstein, J. L., B. S. Simon, and K. C. Salinas. 1997. Involving parents in homework in the middle grades. *Phi Delta Kappan Research Bulletin,* No. 18.

Finn, L. M. 2011. Variation, so meaningful yet so misunderstood—Deming's SoPK Part 111. Posted in The Deming Files, courtesy of the W. Edwards Deming Institute.

Frick, T. W. 1991. *Restructuring education through technology.* Bloomington, IN: Phi Delta Kappa Educational Foundation.

Frick, T. W. 1993. A systems view of restructuring education. In C. M. Reigeluth and B. Banathy (eds.), *Comprehensive Systems Design: A New educational Technology*, pp. 260–271. Berlin: Springer-Verlag.

Fulghum, L. R. 1987. We learned it all in kindergarten, *Reader's Digest*, 131(786): 115.

Fullan, M. 2008. *The six secrets of change.* San Francisco: Jossey-Bass.

Gardner, H.1983. *Frames of mind: The theory of multiple intelligences.* New York: Basic Books.

Gilbert, R. M. 1992. *Extraordinary relationships: A new way of thinking about human interactions.* Minneapolis: Chronimed Publishing.

Goleman, D. P. 1995. *Emotional intelligence: Why it can matter more than IQ for character, health and lifelong achievement.* New York: Bantam Books.

Goodlad, J. I. 1984. *A place called school.* New York: McGraw-Hill Books.

Goodlad, J. I. May 5, 2010. What works and doesn't work in school reform—Part 2 of 3. The Answer Sheet Archive—A School Survival Guide for Parents. *The Washington Post.*

Greenwood, M. S., and H. J. Gaunt. 1994. *Total quality management for schools.* London: Cassell Education.

Gym, H. 2011, June 8. Reformers please listen to what parents want for schools. CNN *Up-Bringing* blog, http://www.cnn.com/2011/OPINION/06/08/gym.schools.parents/index.html?hpt=hp_bn8. Accessed May 7, 2013.

Haidt, J. 2006. *The happiness hypothesis.* New York: Basic Books.

Handy, C. 1997. The search for meaning. *Leader to Leader*, 5: 14–20.

Handy, C. 1995. *The age of paradox.* Boston: Harvard Business Review Press.

Hargreaves, D. 2006. *A new shape for schooling: Deep experience-1.* London: Specialist Schools and Academies Trust.

Hirsch, E. D. 1999. *The schools we need—And why we don't have them.* New York: Anchor Books.

Huizinga, J. 1938. *Homo Ludens: A study of the play element in culture.* London: Roy Publishers.

Illich, I. 1970. *Deschooling society.* San Francisco: Harper and Row Publishers.

Ind, N. 2012. Humble leaders. *RSA Journal,* Summer 2012. RSA.org. http://www.thersa.org/fellowship/journal/archive/summer-2012/features/humble-leaders. Accessed May 7, 2013.

Jackson, M. C. 2003. *Systems thinking: Creative holism for managers.* New York: John Wiley & Sons Ltd.

Jacob, B., and L. Lefgren. 2007. What do parents value in education? An empirical investigation of parents' revealed preferences for teachers. *Quarterly Journal of Economics,* 122: 1603–1607.

Johnston, R., and G. Clark. 2001. *Service operations management.* New York: Pearson Education Ltd.

Kahane, A. 2004. *Solving tough problems.* San Francisco: Berrett-Koehler.

Kanter, R. M. 1989. *When Giants Learn to Dance: the definitive guide to corporate America's changing strategies for success.* Touchstone: Simon & Schuster, Inc.

King, D. 2002. The changing shape of leadership. *Educational Leadership,* 59(8):61–63.

King, K. S., and T. W. Frick. 1999. Transforming education: Case studies in systems thinking. Systems Thinking: The Key to Educational Redesign. Paper presented at the annual meeting of the American Educational Research Association, April 19, Montreal, Canada.

Kofman, F., and P. Senge. 2001. *Communities of commitment: the heart of learning organizations.* Cambridge: Organizational Learning Center, Massachusetts Institute of Technology.

Kohn, A. 1999. *Punished by rewards: The trouble with gold stars, incentive plans, A's, praise, and other bribes.* Boston: Houghton Mifflin Company.

Kotter, J. P. 1996. *Leading change.* Boston: Harvard Business School Press.

Langford, D. P., and B. A. Cleary. 1995. *Orchestrating learning with quality.* Milwaukee: ASQC Quality Press.

Levin, H. L., G. V. Glass, and G. R. Meister. 1987. Cost-effectiveness of computer-assisted instruction. *Evaluation Review* 11:50, online at http://erx.sagepub.com/content/11/1/50. doi: 10.1177/0193841X8701100103.

Lewin, R. 2001. *Complexity—Life at the edge of chaos.* Chicago: University of Chicago.

Lounsbury, J. H. 2009. Deferred but not deterred: A middle school manifesto. *Middle School Journal,* 40(5):31–36.

Lovelock, J. 1979. *Gaia—A new look at life on Earth.* London: Oxford University Press.

Lunenberg, F. C. 2010. Total quality management applied to schools. *Schooling,* 1(1). http://www.nationalforum.com/Electronic%20Journal%20Volumes/Lunenburg,%20Fred%20C.%20Total%20Quality%20Management%20Applied%20to%20Schools%20Schooling%20V1%20N1%202010.pdf. Accessed May 7, 2013.

Maccia, E., and G. Maccia. 1966. *Development of educational theory derived from three models.* Project No. 5-0368. Washington, D.C: US Office of Education.

Maslow, A. H. 1943. A theory of human motivation. *Psychological Review* 50(4): 370-96.

Maslow, A. 1954. *Motivation and personality.* New York: Harper.

McCrae, R. R. 2007. Aesthetic skills as a universal marker of openness to experience. *Motivation and Emotion,* 31(1):5–11.

Meadows, D. H. 2009. *Thinking in systems—A primer.* London: Taylor & Francis.

Mlodinow, L., 2012. *Subliminal: The revolution of the new unconscious and what it teaches us about ourselves.* London: Allen Lane.

Murgatroyd, S. May 2010. Wicked problems and the work of the school. *Live and Learn,* 17. http://www.etfliveandlearn.eu/issue/may/2010/59/wicked-problems-and-the-work-of-the-school/english. Accessed May 7, 2013.

National Alliance for Secondary Education and Transition. National standards and quality indicators: Transition toolkit for systems improvement. www.NASETalliance.org.

National College of School Leadership 2012. Leadership and developing parental engagement: A tool to help you audit and improve your practice. National College of School Leadership: www.ncsl.org.uk. URI: http://dera.ioe.ac.uk/id/eprint/10430.

National Commision on Excellence in Education (ECEE). 1983. A nation at risk: The importance of educational reform. www.ed.gov/pubs/NatAtRisk/index.html.

Nevis, E. C., J. E. Lancourt, and H. G. Vassallo. 1996. *Intentional revolutions: A seven-point strategy for transforming organizations.* San Francisco: Jossey-Bass.

Orbach, S. 2012. The sad truth. *RSA Journal,* Spring.

Pasmore, W. A. 1988. *Designing effective organizations: The socio-technical systems perspective.* New York: Wiley & Sons.

Pirsig, R. M. 2006. *Zen and the art of motorcycle maintenance: An inquiry into values.* New York: HarperCollins.

Ravitch, D. 2012. Schools we can envy. *The New York Review of Books*, 59(18). http://www.nybooks.com/articles/archives/2012/mar/08/schools-we-can-envy/?pagination=false. Accessed May 7, 2013.

Reigeluth, C. M. 1994. Introduction: The imperative for systemic change. In C. Reigeluth and R. Garfinkle (eds.), *Systemic Change in Education* (pp. 3–11). Englewood Cliffs, NJ: Educational Technology Publications.

Reigeluth, C. M. 2006. A leveraged emergent approach to systemic transformation. *Tech Trends*, 50(2), 46–47.

Reigeluth, C. M., and R. J. Garfinkle. 1994. *Systemic change in education.* Englewood Cliffs, NJ: Educational Technology Publications.

Rittel, H., and M. Webber. 1973. Dilemmas in a general theory of planning. *Policy Sciences*, 4:155–169.

Rockwell, S. 1997. Mentoring through accessible, authentic opportunities. *Preventing School Failure*, 3(41): 111–114.

Seddon, J. 2008. *Systems thinking in the public sector: The failure of the reform regime and a manifesto for a better way.* Devon, UK: Triarchy Press.

Seddon, J. 2013. The back-office: A train crash coming to a town near you. In Seddon, J., *Delivering Public Services That Work: Volume 2.* London: Triarchy Press.

Senge, P. M. 1994. *The fifth discipline fieldbook: Strategies and tools for building a learning organization.* New York: Crown Business.

Senge, P. M. 2006. *The fifth discipline: The art and practices of the learning organization*, 2nd ed. New York: Random House.

Senge, P., N. Cambron-McCabe, T. Lucas, B. Smith, J. Dutton, and A. Kleiner. 2000. *Schools that learn: A fifth discipline fieldbook for educators, parents, and everyone who cares about education.* New York: Doubleday.

Shenk, D. 2010. *The genius in all of us: New insights into genetics, talent, and IQ.* Anchor Books, a division of Random House, NY.

Sherwood, D. 2002. *Seeing the forest for the trees—A manager's guide to applying systems thinking.* Boston: Nicolas Brealey Publishing.

Shukla, M. 1994. Why corporations fail. *Productivity* 34(4): 629–639.

Sizer, T. 1984. *Horace's compromise: The dilemma of the American high school.* Boston: Houghton Mifflin.

Smith, M. K. 2001. Chris Argyris: Theories of action, double-loop learning and organizational learning. *The encyclopaedia of informal education.* www.infed.org/thinkers/argyris.htm. Accessed May 7, 2013.

Steiner E. 1988. *Methodology of theory building.* Sydney: Educology Research Associates.

Stevens, R. 1983. *Erik Erikson: An introduction.* New York: St. Martin's.

Stoll, L., R. Bolam, A. McMahon, M. Wallace, and S. Thomas. 2006. Professional learning communities: A review of the literature. *Journal of Educational Change*, 7(4):221–258.

Swanson, C. B. 2004. *Who graduates? Who doesn't? A statistical portrait of public high school graduation, Class of 2001.* Washington, DC: The Urban Institute.

Thornburg, D. D. 1995. Welcome to the communications age. *Internet Research*, 5(1): 64–70.

Townsel, K. T. 1997. Mentoring African American youth. *Preventing School Failure*, 41(3):125–127.

Trivers, R. 2011. *The folly of fools—The logic of deceit and self-deception in human life.* London: Basic Books.

Turkle, S. 2011. *Alone together: Why we expect more from technology and less from each other.* New York: Basic Books.

Tyack, D., and L. Cuban. 1995. *Tinkering toward Utopia—A century of public school reform.* Cambridge, MA: Harvard University Press.

Tyack, D., and L. Cuban. 2004. Excerpts from a conversation at the Askwith Education Forum, Harvard Graduate School of Education, *HGSE News.*

Tymms, P., and Merrell, C. 2011. Improving attainment across a whole district: School reform through peer tutoring in a randomized controlled trial. *School effectiveness and school improvement: An international journal of research, policy and practice* 22(3).

Usher, R., and I. Bryant. 1989. *Adult education as theory, practice and research.* London: Routledge.

Vidal, G. 2004. *Imperial America: Reflections on the United States of Amnesia.* New York: Nation Books.

Vygotsky, L. S. 1978. Mind in society: The development of higher psychological processes. Harvard University Press.

Wadham, L. 2009. *The secret life of France.* London: Faber and Faber.

Warner, J. 2005. *Perfect madness—Motherhood in an age of anxiety.* London: Penguin Group.

Warner, J. 2012. Why American kids are brats. *Time Ideas,* Feb. 10. http://ideas.time.com/2012/02/10/why-american-kids-are-brats/. Accessed May 7, 2013.

Wheatley, M. J. 1999. Bringing schools back to life. Schools as living systems. In *Creating Successful Schools: Voices from the University, the Field, and the Community.* Norwood, MA: Christopher-Gordon Publishers. MargaretWheatley.com. http://www.margaretwheatley.com/articles/lifetoschools.html. Accessed May 7, 2013.

Wheatley, M. J. 2004. Is the pace of life hindering our ability to manage? *Management Today,* March. MargaretWheatley.com. http://www.margaretwheatley.com/articles/thepaceoflife.html. Accessed May 7, 2013.

Wheatley, M. J. 2006. *Leadership and the new science—Discovering order in a chaotic world.* San Francisco: Berrett-Koehler.

Womack, J. P., D. T. Jones, and D. Roos. 1990. *The machine that changed the world: The story of lean production.* Yorkshire, UK: Rawson Associates.

Zohar, D., and I. Marshall. 2001. *Spiritual intelligence: The ultimate intelligence.* New York: Bloomsbury.

Index